ZERO DAY
ZERO BUDGET

ZERO DAY
ZERO BUDGET

Information Security Management Beyond Standards

Imre Farkas

ISBN: 9781097574179

FIRST EDITION

zerodayzerobudget.com

This book is dedicated to all those who go above and beyond to make our digital future safe to live in.

So, this book is dedicated to YOU, and to your success!

CONTENTS

INTRODUCTION

A blacksmith making swords two thousand years ago was a specialist. He would, however, likely not need to address issues as complex we are facing today, so for a blacksmith, being a "narrow specialist" was the way to go. On the other hand, the blacksmith learning about arts, or other matters not directly related to his "field" would probably stand out in terms of the quality and appeal of his product against his peers. For us, today's security management professionals, such "extra" appears to be more and more an essential element of success. There is so much know-how, so much information, and it can be so confusing that, often these days, someone, merely using common sense, appears to be a genius. Just think about it. One great example is the plethora of risk assessment methodologies. The fancier and more intricate they became, the more confusing and cumbersome they were (and still are) to apply, and getting a relevant, practical and actionable result is all the less likely.

You want to protect your company from security risks, create visibility and credibility for security, and achieve lasting improvement in the security posture of your organization. For that you need to drive significant change, small change, take ownership or push ownership, delegate, cooperate, integrate, but are met with delays, complacency, lack of budget and resources, lousy attitude, feeling overwhelmed, new attacks and risks, too many audit findings, low board-level priority of security, stakeholders not grasping your messages. You are applying "best practices" and "control measures" appropriately to "threat scenarios" and "risks" — and you are still feeling stuck? I promise that in this book, you'll find some answers, while we figure out why all that happens, and I share my experience on how to overcome all that.

Whether you are an experienced security professional or manager, just starting in the field of information security, or "migrating" from another professional area, in this book I aim to provide useful experience, insights and practices, with relevant context. The goal being to help you operate in this environment with success and fulfillment. Why aren't all the standards, methodologies and other books enough, so that I had to write this book? Quite honestly, I have found that this kind of knowledge is either missing, or very well hidden in those, and so, it is quite difficult to obtain. At least, for me, it took almost twenty years. They say, "By-the-book is for the book" —

I think not in this case.

Looking at the chapter titles, you may wonder what most of the topics have to do with security. Applying them to our profession will likely seem counterintuitive at first. However, that is the whole point of the book; looking outside the box! Security people want to deal with security and not with economics, psychology, and all the other stuff this book is about. But what is security really about? It's about risks, vulnerabilities, firewalls, anti-malware protection, mainly technical things, right? Sure, but security is also about economics, psychology, people, politics, communication, the smaller or larger organization itself, it's clients and suppliers. Security is about all that "other" stuff as well. Also, last, but not least, common sense.

Read on and take your mind and soul on a journey which may change your perspective on what your chosen profession actually is — forever!

PHASE ONE

ALIGN

NOTE ONE
on Starting Out

"Orientation Express"

WHEN JOINING A NEW COMPANY, team or client organization there is always a great deal of new information to be absorbed, and getting up to speed and becoming productive fast requires a strategy and a set of useful tactics. Such new information ranges from the organization's structure (i.e., who is who) to the business itself and its priorities, from the regulatory environment to the IT infrastructure, processes and all the elements of the security program already in place. You must be able to recognize the missing pieces of information as well, to identify blind spots which inevitably occur.

No one will babysit you

The amount and complexity of this information will vary. Trying to absorb all you need to know in an unstructured way is always overwhelming. Also, the more senior your new position is, the less information is readily available; delivered by your boss or volunteered by your peers. If you take on a security analyst job, you will likely be provided with a sufficient amount of guidance to start operating fairly effectively after a few weeks. Taking over a security management position though is tougher; no one has time to babysit you! Several weeks may pass until you stop feeling utterly lost. Anticipate and prepare for this period, and put it to good use!

This predicament is particularly common in the consultancy business, where it's routine to run multiple engagements with multiple clients at the same time, and regularly start new engagements, encounter new environments. In most instances, you are required to hit the ground running at a new company or in a new role. Even if you are in the same position for several years, the quickly changing environment where you are required to perform will always challenge you. So being able to orient oneself in new situations is an essential skill — you lose more time and momentum in such situations than you may realize.

Getting practical

So what would be the most effective way to orient yourself with lightning speed, so that you can actually start delivering results and have peace of mind as well? The following methods worked great for me during my consulting engagements, as well as whenever I landed in a new position at the same or a new company.

First of all, gain some perspective. Get to as high in the organization as possible to obtain information about the company's values, vision, strategic goals, and operational plans. At this point, it is quite tempting to keep to ourselves at our desk and read all we can in the documentation provided to us, and, worst of all, stay within our department or division for information. When it comes to making decisions, however, the lack of perspective and the understanding of the bigger picture, the commonly accepted principles and viewpoints of other parts of the organization, will lead to misjudgment of priorities and result in wrong decisions. Often, after several months, it's just a feeling of being stuck, not progressing due to decisions beyond your control, making no apparent sense. That is because you most probably lack the perspective of the decision-makers. You may not even have had any meaningful conversations with them, and you perceive only your side of the story. Knowing just one account is dangerous though.[1] Recognize that and act to change it. You may call this empathy too.

Being familiar with broader organizational plans will also help prevent another issue, materializing after 6 to 12 months after starting a role, which is becoming reactive. Even if one has grand plans to enhance security, the world moves on constantly. A solution specified a few months ago may not fit the current plans anymore and that will quickly push a security manager and his/her team into reactive mode. You are always reacting, never leading — when there are quite a few ways for a security team to be on the leading edge of transforming a business. More on that later.

Another inhibitor is a lack of structured information. To address that, peruse organization charts, audit reports, even find and evaluate asset inventories. It is vital not to be shy in asking for and obtaining these documents. The level of preparedness, detail, and currency are a pretty good indication of the overall maturity of the organization, giving you additional insight into what to expect and how to proceed.

Everyone's brain works differently. For that reason, all the information you obtain in a new situation will only make real sense if it is organized according to how your brain understands the world. Use mind-maps as a means to organize all that data. Even if you are not a visual person, the freely definable structure of mind-maps is a great advantage in understanding, recalling, and also gaining deeper insights into more extensive sets of unstructured or differently structured information.

Don't hide

The most obvious tip: Talk to people! Being more of an introvert myself, that bit had been particularly hard for me. Some people are naturally good at engaging people and starting a conversation. As for me, I have always felt a bit cumbersome in the social realm, so I devised some ways to make this challenge easier. First, adopting the mindset that I was there to learn and not to teach made all the difference. Initially, and later on as well, one can be much more productive by not preaching to people about security. Now, that means you should do less talking and much-much more listening. Now comes the tricky part: how do you get people to talk to you so you can listen? Well, by asking questions. I don't mean to ask questions randomly though — this is where security standards and other structured (but generic!) knowledge comes into play. Adopting an auditor's mindset in discovering how things work helps a lot. (Hint: searching the Web for "auditing XYZ activity" will yield very different, and much better, more relevant results than searching just for "XYZ activity". When learning about a particular environment, the methods for your investigations, produced by the latter combination of search phrases, are radically more helpful! Asking questions, especially if that is not in your nature, can be difficult. It can be started by leaving your ego at the door and saying *"I'm still new here, so can you help me understand X or Y...?"*. People usually love to tell you their version or opinion. Collect as many "versions" as you can.

Find your allies

Find thought leaders and influencers inside the organization. The people shaping how things are done, are often not formally appointed leaders, but key people with lots of experience — and influence. Get them to talk to you, and later on, talk to them to get their buy-in. They are the ones who can tell you about the history of the company, and why things are the way they are today.

It is essential not to make any judgments at this point — at least not to the face of people you are interviewing. No one likes a wise-guy. On the contrary, it is best to see the good in all you are hearing (granted, that may be hard sometimes) and make people feel good about themselves — not necessarily about their results (especially if they go against your ideas), but about being helpful and giving you their time in this crucial initial period. Also, people you will meet will likely have invested considerable effort into arriving where they are now. Also, the foundation of any partnership is finding common ground. Now is the time to do that.

This initial learning phase is the time to find out what success looks like and according to what principles it is measured and evaluated by your boss, other leaders of the organization, and your peers as well. Getting viewpoints from line-of-business leaders, managers is critical, as security must align with and support business goals. Also, listening to people from all around the broader organization will reveal the best structure for building your approach, ways, and language for delivering your personal views. I have found that one of the biggest reasons for failure is not listening, either out of arrogance or a perceived lack of time. Having a sense of urgency in actions shouldn't mean cutting before you measure! Rushing ahead at the expense of defining clear, commonly understood and agreed success criteria is a recipe for failure.

Relations are established during the first months and *going forward people will remember not your particular achievements, but the nature of their relationship with you.*

Do you often send emails to people you've never met, even though you work in the same building every day? That is not the optimal way to introduce yourself. The best approach, if at all possible due to geographical reasons or timezone differences, is just to visit a new peer, colleague, or someone who has been with the organization a while but you've never met, in person. The effectiveness of written communication in itself is only a fraction of that of interacting face to face. You need to introduce yourself in person whenever possible. The impact is much more profound, and you can develop rapport.

You do need and will likely have some time for orientation, but invariably you will be expected to perform after some time. Don't wait for your boss to come to you asking what you have been doing for the last three months. Get ahead. Write down your goals, and even if you do not commit to them in writing to your boss, do commit to yourself to have a list of achievements by the end of the first three months, or 100 days. Many good books are collecting "the first 100 days" for leaders. Psst! Those books are not strictly for CEOs or executives!

Another thing: do your homework, *don't be lazy* and read through and understand all your standards, references, relevant internal policies. *You must know what you are talking about, otherwise your input will be meaningless.*

Devising, specifying, and delivering a relevant security agenda and becoming a real partner for your business is only possible after arming yourself with organization-specific knowledge. Learn, specify, and then deliver.

NOTE TWO
on Service

"From newcomer to business partner"

ONCE YOU FEEL CONFIDENT in your role, you shouldn't. That is
the point where business-as-usual activities start to become
routine, and it looks like you are filling your role admirably.
That is the state, though, where many practitioners begin to
feel content in their position and cease looking for new information. I did that a few times myself. There are, however, a
bunch of landmines still to be discovered and avoided, such as
the *real* role and perception of the security department across
the organization.

Less May Be More

The information security function is frequently identified as
one that makes up and then enforces security requirements.
We are faced with the inadequacy of this approach daily, yet
we seem to be stuck with it. Security and control requirements

are not just made up – they are generally defined and implemented following a particular standard or methodology. However, over-reliance on such extraneous information may well lead us to believe we have done everything we can and so will curb our capabilities to protect and support our organization as security professionals. There are several additional factors to consider, both internal and external; among the most significant ones are the priorities, goals, needs, and even culture of our organization. Any security initiative or protective measure not aligned with those will inevitably suffer.

For instance, we all know the fret caused by overly cumbersome sets of authentication rules (a case in point is the notorious discontent around "password complexity" rules, if you have them, that is). The moment people – your users – feel their work is impeded in any way by some security rule, they will inevitably find ways to go around it to make their lives easier. That is to be expected and completely natural. However, in the end, it undermines security, at times making the situation even worse than without that particular security rule.

Consequently, measures forced onto an organization will eventually fail to deliver the expected result. They may have other, unintended consequences, like frustration, resistance or even sabotage though. Enforcement does not work without persuasion (or incentives). Think twice before pushing a new rule without consultation with appropriate stakeholders.

Plan to Serve

Let's see how we can prevent such fiascos and transform them into easy successes. All right, "easy success" is a bit of an exaggeration. "Better chance of success" is a more appropriate expectation to set. To overcome this issue, what you need is a good understanding of our organization's goals and transform security from an inhibiting factor, a necessary evil – the necessity of which is also not always so apparent either – into an object of desire. Again "desire" is a bit exaggerated, but that is on purpose. We do not merely want to get by, or improve things a little – we want to make a difference — right? The approach where you listen before you speak may transform security itself into service.

The term "service" in this instance is not meant to refer to the practice of outsourcing our security operations to external providers. Instead, it serves to emphasize the positive approach in defining our reason to exist in our organization as a security team.

IT Service Management is (on paper, for sure) a well-established practice, with its foundations laid down by ITIL.[2] On the security front, however, there is a substantial lag in this regard. One of the reasons is most likely the lack of practical guidance. The current versions of relevant ISO standards[3] or COBIT have[4] taken noticeable steps toward the mindset of focusing on creating and protecting "business value." A great example of this is an ITGI publication called The Business Model for Information Security (BMIS), later integrated into COBIT 5. The standalone paper itself is still very much a worthwhile read in itself as it provides a well structured if theoretical, context for security programs. It is an excellent compilation of the "what" in terms of operating in a service-oriented and customer-focused security function. The "why" however is still lacking.

These resources and those who apply them as well are still somewhat biased toward control and compliance. So even though I'm sure their intentions are not such, yet most practitioners using them still consider them as boxes to tick — security for the sake of security (or compliance). However, it all depends on the mindset of the reader. I am confident that revisiting well-known sources of security practices after reading this book, you will discover new patterns which only reveal themselves in a very particular context — the context of service orientation. Even an audit engagement, commonly considered a drain on operational resources of the audited area, can be designed and executed with a service mindset; producing drastically different results for the audited area, the auditors, management and the whole organization itself.

When applying the principle of business partnership, it becomes quite apparent, that all facets of security, including awareness are closely tied together; the key to hardening the human firewall, for instance, is good security "service." People, after all, like to be served. Still, information security keeps saying 'No' to quite a few business ideas or initiatives or makes it a hassle in subtle, or not so subtle ways, in the name of security. Also, however counterproductive, that seems to become more and more prevalent. After all, as the saying goes, the most secure computer is one locked away, enclosed in a concrete block, disconnected from power and network. However, this approach is not forward-looking and very far from what you would call "business-oriented."

Ask and You Shall Receive — Answers

Figuring out how to best integrate into and serve our organization as a security team is difficult. One of the best tools to employ for this purpose is conducting surveys. There is a lot to be learned from them.

Analyzing the results of several such internal surveys I have conducted over time in different organizations on different levels of organizational and security process maturity, I have found that there are some recurring themes. These surveys were conducted among the organization's middle management, and different groups of the organization that were in a regular working relationship with the security team, and, of course, among end-users. Perhaps not surprisingly, many of the concerns raised by survey respondents were related to their own experience working with or being "controlled" by the security team, hence subjective. But that is all right as a good security mindset can only be adopted by a satisfied (or at least not frustrated) user base and peer group. The main points highlighted by the survey analyses were the following.

- Proactivity and business partnership (need more of)
- Response time to inquiries, as it relates to operational requests (like access requests) or project level cooperation (faster)
- More straightforward and unambiguous security policies
- Transparency of security procedures (i.e., What is required from me, as an end-user and what can I expect from the security team to gain access to a resource or validate a system specification)

You can catch instances where such service mindset is missing when you or your colleagues are always waiting for the other team, waiting for the information you missed to include somewhere — but are not proactively seeking it out. The most effective approach is to look at your security function as a "business inside the business." With such a mindset, all the activities appearing superfluous inside an organization, such as doing strategic and financial planning, marketing, communication, will all begin to make sense!

NOTE THREE
on Strategy and Governance

"Future-proofing your actions"

SERVICE MINDSET, PARTNERSHIP — what do these have to do with information security? Just put yourself in the shoes of your top management. How much time and resources would you allocate to an activity you see the benefits of and compared to that, how much to things you have never heard of and are as obscure as a next-gen firewall, virtual infrastructure or cloud security?

To become a real partner, you need oversight and confidence in your words and actions, and that can only come from a comprehensive view of everything you are or should be, doing. Organizations and security offices may have several kinds of critical periods during their life cycle. Such critical phases are, for example, the initial setup of a security organization, merger and acquisition activities or reorganizations. These critical times are when we need the confidence of having a good oversight of our activities in security. During business-as-usual operations, the quality of oversight often becomes secondary. Staying the course and keeping our ability to steer our activities is even more important during times of business-as-usual, though — if you are lucky enough to see such days. If not, still, I would allocate at least 20% of my time to think ahead.

Strategic planning and governance are quite elusive concepts to many a good security practitioner. Practically, however, these are just a series of steps one needs to take, to arrive at a set of broad but relevant and actionable long or medium-term goals and plans, and the organizational structures, procedures, roles, and activities needed to achieve those goals. In other words, strategic planning and governance are just processes you need to define and execute. As such, they have inputs, steps, roles and outputs, among other process attributes described later.

In any busy organization, the security officer has their hands full all the time, reacting to cyberattacks, audit findings, evaluating security measures of new business initiatives, performing security reviews of systems and applications, and a myriad of other important activities.

There is, in fact, a distinct meaning to "important activities", which is worth examining, to understand two key things — first, some basic principles of time management, second, an important realization about "activities".

You have two kinds of problems: the urgent ones and the important ones. The urgent are not important, and the important are never urgent.[5] As any basic time management methodology will tell you, defining what you focus on at any given moment, should be determined by these two attributes.

That will lead to four basic categories of tasks, neither urgent nor important, urgent but not important, not urgent but important and both urgent and important. Think of this as a two by two matrix. Urgent problems (important or not) are the realm of incident management in the security world, that is quite obvious. If we drop problems neither urgent nor important form our todo list, which we should, we are left, for our current discussion, with the not urgent but important things. Strategic planning most definitely falls into this category.

The apparent lack of urgency of strategic planning deceives us into ignoring it altogether, and that leads us to a bad place: nowhere. It is best to adopt the simplified approach quoted above and realize that strategic planning is so important, it should be our priority. Today. Not tomorrow — today!

The realization about strategic planning being an activity is, that if we neglect defining what we want to achieve by strategic planning, we may be very busy — going nowhere, fast. And that is also true when we operate without a strategic plan. Never confuse activity with accomplishment!

What we want out of a strategic plan is to be relevant, actionable, and controllable. We may call this the *RAC triangle of strategy.* Just a fun mnemonic for those who are familiar with the CIA triad of information security — I sure hope you are!

A fundamental element of strategic planning is to distinguish between different types of goals and activities, in terms of their impact, resource needs, and most importantly, their time horizon. Most of the time, we would separate strategic initiatives ("big rocks"), tactical implementations (I would call these "projects") and operational activities. It is important to recognize that tactical steps will only have any discernible effect in the next quarter or beyond, and strategic moves will likely not yield any benefit until next year! That means it may be a long time before we find out whether we were right. So it is all the more important to take Michael Porter's view to heart, that "The essence of strategy is choosing what not to do."

When formulating our information security strategy, it is quite tempting to prioritize initiatives that address the list of audit findings. On the other hand, I have seen fundamental security flaws "floating around" in audit reports for 2 to 3 years without the root cause ever addressed. Closing gaps and reducing risks highlighted by internal or external audits is, of course, a valid aim for any department. It should not, however, be the end goal in and of itself, and the list of audit findings should definitely not be our only list of actions, let alone the sole input defining risk in our strategic planning for security.

The inclination to tailor our strategy around risks highlighted by audits is different in various industries. Compared to industries and sectors lacking direct government regulation for security and control environment, in regulated industries — such as financial services, telecommunication, healthcare — audits performed by both an internal audit function and external parties such as regulators, certification bodies and other authorities are stricter and more frequent. That increases pressure for compliance.

Also, keep in mind that the value of audit findings for the strategic planning of information security depends largely on the maturity of the auditing bodies themselves. At its infant stage of maturity, an audit will look for, find, and address only symptoms. More advanced auditing firms or departments adopt a risk and process-based approach and will evaluate not only the effectiveness of controls but control design (policies) and the sustainability of the controls as well (do they last or fall out of daily practice over time).

Strategic initiatives must have a proper business case and make economic sense to have any kind of impression on top management. That is probably the hardest nut for a security guy to crack. See if you find some ideas in the further chapters, particularly the one on Finance.

Our strategy should formalize what the most appropriate security goals are, given the mission and goals of our company, and what the right things to do for us, as the security team, are to achieve those goals. According to well-established definitions, good governance is about ensuring we are doing the right things, and we are doing them the right way. Okay, so the "right things" would be defined by our strategy. The "right way" part, however, is very easy to overlook, meaning we may be less concerned about the "how," about establishing and maintaining a good security governance structure. After all, our organization has its own way of doing things, from getting business cases approved, to running and controlling projects, defining organizational structures, performing audits, management reporting, etc. Or it doesn't. Either way, following the ways of our company will provide a level of comfort where extra optimization efforts will seem unnecessary and even counterproductive. They are not!

In many executives' minds, "governance" is synonymous with "compliance" and auditing. That misconception is likely driven by the pressures of regulators, clients, and other mainly external parties. These external parties put pressure on organizations to provide assurance of adequate control measures to mitigate risks and exposures to the company and, more importantly, its clients and employees in terms of security and privacy. Accounting, safety and a multitude of other areas not even covered here. Audit and self-assessment reports are the means to show our compliance to parties both external and internal. But the pressure to demonstrate compliance often limits our thinking and relegates the achievement of "real" security to the "pet projects" of the security manager, being worked on only as secondary priorities. Unless of course, we are clever enough to link the two. You can only be effective by establishing proper governance structures and practices — not merely striving to be compliant.

It's easy to find the basics of security governance with a quick search on the Internet, but let me just point out some key questions I usually have, that will help to map out your organization's governance structures and to align with them.

- What are the ways the organization defines business value/benefits?
- How is resource allocation achieved in the organizational matrix?
- What kind of performance management is in place?
- How does the organization manage programs and projects?
- Are there any formally defined "programs" or "projects" at all?
- How will you be able to align your structured security approach to whatever is standard practice for enterprise-level risk management at the company?
- How will you make way for your initiatives if there is no standard practice at the company around project and program management?

It is quite common for companies to have some kind of governance framework for running and transforming their own business. Any organization worth their salt has already introduced some sort of project management methodology, plugged into their corporate governance structure, even if it's not practiced across the board. A way to introduce change into an organization is a very basic survival tool in the information age. Connecting with top-level decision-making forums justifies this and gives power to such arrangements. Without aligning project and program management activities with top management's ways of operation will quickly make any security-related projects created, irrelevant.

But coming back to the original question, in the lack of formal and working project/program/portfolio management, we must turn to much more unstructured ways of advancing the security agenda. That is the situation, where the tools for dealing with company culture, politics, marketing and selling and sometimes even making hard decisions autonomously, come into play. IT and security governance methods originate from corporate governance, which originated from state governance which is closely linked with, or embedded into, politics.

Governance, as a methodical discipline is on the "light side" of the political toolbox. But other factors may have adverse effects on our success, factors residing on the "dark side" of politics. If governance is part of good politics, what kind of invisible dark magic lies beyond governance methods, on the "dark side" of politics, that has such a fundamental effect on us when we operate as part of an organization? In the next chapter, we use our x-ray vision to find out.

NOTE FOUR
on Politics

"Developing your X-ray vision"

OPERATING IN A CORPORATE ENVIRONMENT is full of challenges that are quite apparent from the outset. That is, however, only the tip of the iceberg, as the real driving forces and inhibiting factors lie beneath the surface. As a security "field agent," you must develop your night vision, or even x-ray vision to identify those invisible internal forces influencing your effectiveness.

We all have our views about politicians. Politics and diplomacy though, are in fact professions in their own right, and there are some lessons we can learn from them.

There are aspects which I call the "dark side" of politics. Whereas the "light side" focuses on creating order from chaos (i.e., governance), the "dark side" recognizes that we are only human — smart individually but so simple-minded in large numbers, also mostly driven by self-interest.

One of the main inhibitors of progressing a security program may be the power plays different colleagues and departments may be stuck playing, due to the lack of universally understood and accepted common priorities. That might even happen without any malicious or (overly) selfish attitudes too.

Also, without an overall governance structure, leaders of different parts of a large organization, and members of disjointed management forums may have a partial or completely mistaken view of how decisions are made. They may be led to believe that decisions made at a particular forum will be directly implemented, whereas, in reality, another (lateral or higher) decision forum is calling the shots. If you lack the full perspective, your expectations will be unrealistic. Such situations are more frequent than you might think, mainly as many organizations are in constant transformation, removing gaps or redundancies — but creating new ones in the process. Besides, the official organization chart often does not tell you the whole story about who the real influencers are.

Such forces reveal themselves when you start asking questions such as:

- Who are the real influencers and decision-makers? (Sometimes asking directly is the way to go.)
- What kind of relations are at play among members of management and people in key influencing roles?
- How is decision making done in practice?
- What preparations are needed for a security initiative to be considered by management? Are you tied to planning cycles?
- Do you need a formal business case or financial impact analysis?
- What is the governing body prioritizing initiatives on the

company (or even just on IT) level?

- Quite importantly: What does the complete program or project portfolio look like on company (corporate), or IT level?

- How formal is the organization in reality? (Are you able to achieve more by approaching key people informally first? — The answer is 'Yes' in 99% of the cases, so practice your elevator speech!)

The term awareness "campaign" originates from politics. The communication channels you pick to deliver your security awareness messages will significantly impact the effectiveness of your broadcasting effort. It's worthwhile to study how some of the most successful political campaigns were done. Study the methods used, but not necessarily the mindset behind those "over-promise/under-deliver" campaigns.

In modern history, some of the most notable innovators in terms of campaigning can be remembered from the USA: Richard Nixon used the mass communication medium called the radio, to win, John F. Kennedy was the first "TV president", and Barack Obama harnessed Facebook's power to raise funding and facilitate his constituents' self-organization, as well as Donald Trump, who took to Twitter to broadcast messages to more than 55 million people — directly. The methods of the parties or civilians in the "opposition" party are quite interesting as well, mainly as they are usually able to obtain less funding.

What can you do if you lack funding and power? You become an activist! Grassroots organizers' main goal is to recruit a large number of following, to challenge and change the status quo.[6] Now once you have a following, you can influence their behavior in different ways. Instead of trying to brainwash people with security "propaganda," look for issues they have with the current security measures. Why not turn security functionality into a selling point? You can, for instance, explain that employees are required to remember a multitude of passwords because you lack the funding for a single sign-on (SSO)[7] solution. This approach would make people "want" an SSO. Previously I shared results of surveys I have performed in the past. Now I call you to launch your investigation. Ask your end-users to find out what kind of impact current security features have on their *"security experience,"* and what kind of improvement it would mean to introduce different, enhanced solutions or procedures. Use targeted questions to guide the discussion, or open questions to get "real" answers, such as:

- "How much loss of time or productivity do you experience due to multiple log-ons needed?"
- "Do you think a single-sign-on solution would make your life easier and make you more productive?"
- "How much time do you spend (waste?) with [insert security feature here]?"
- "How do security and control measures impact your productivity in general? Please give a few examples!"

The result of a well-formulated survey should reveal some real business and productivity benefits to be gained (next to the potential risks it is meant to address) by some of the security improvements on your agenda. You are already aware of these potential benefits for sure, but *can you imagine how much more powerful can the voice of hundreds of people can be, than only your own*? Of course, such an interactive approach needs proper preparations with end-users and top management alike. For end-users to respond to such surveys, you would best offer some kind of incentive. Also, management needs to be fully aware of the risk profile of the organization — so they don't remove security functionality and the security department altogether after getting the wrong idea, seeing the amount of lost productivity due to some poorly implemented security measures!

This straightforward approach can and should be supported by many one-on-one discussions with your peers — or peers of your boss, for that matter — inside the organization.

Gathering and understanding the points of view of people you want to influence is invaluable, because "you don't call for a vote unless you have the votes."[8] Let's move on to how you influence decision-makers — after listening to them.

PHASE TWO

JUSTIFY

NOTE FIVE
on Context and Maturity

"Growing up and showing the value of security"

WHY IS IT THAT MOST COMPANIES today have security solutions which are not getting questioned by management and are an accepted part of the cost of operations? Budget items related to these things are taken for granted and do not require extensive business cases for them to be re-justified each year. That is great, but then there are the new solutions, which get ever more sophisticated and for which you have to jump through hoops of fire to gain approval even though in the security practitioner's mind they are just as fundamental today as these well-known "basic" solutions have been for decades. What's happening?

Examples of the former would be firewalls in general or the endpoint security solutions as of today.[9] Do you, or even top management, question the relevance of an endpoint solution today? If not, why? Have solutions that have been around for decades proven their worth? Or, have we got used to them providing a sense of security? Or, do we keep them around without questioning their relevance? These are all valid questions I think, but the main focus of this chapter is to highlight that some security solutions (and their costs) are often readily accepted while others are still not — and we can use this dynamic of the former group to drive adoption of the latter.

What if I tell you that XYZ solution will protect the integrity of personal customer information by applying machine learning and distributed neural networks? What if you try to explain this to a business executive? The result is mostly confusion and ultimately, rejection of the concept of something that is way too complex and seemingly not worth the cost and effort.

What if I tell you that XYZ solution is the "next antivirus," but it is a self-improving defense against data falsification and fraud? Likely that puts my message in a familiar context, where benefits are significantly more transparent, much better communicated and understood. Better yet, if we are prepared with some statistics, preferably from our own organization or our industry. It is quite useful to seek reputable statistics and reports regularly — they will contain facts and compiled information about security breaches and other vital areas. Even though they are mostly compiled by security vendors and consulting firms, still, they are a great resource to use for putting your company's risk profile into context and make threats and benefits more tangible for stakeholders. The caveat here is that only an apples-to-apples comparison should be made; using relevant statistics and fundamentally sound analogies. If our newly proposed solution is not really "the next antivirus" we'd be better off finding a parallel that fits. In the case of a data leakage protection software, it would be probably a proper analogy.

Another approach is to broaden our view such that the new security measure is positioned neither merely as a technology solution looking for a problem, nor an over-formalized procedure. A bigger picture view of the solution will add the context necessary for all players to make sense of it and recognize its benefits. That can yield a much broader consensus; more stakeholders can be identified and consequently, with the right messages, converted into supporters. As an example of this, I tell the story of the HR department turned from opponent to advocate of our new identity management system, in the chapter on Persistence.

Broadening our view of risks, benefits, and solutions to a higher organizational level is even more useful considering the entirety of our security program. The more mature our approach to security, the more benefit it can provide. "Maturity" as a concept for processes and frameworks has been around for decades, originally laid out in the CMMI[10] which has now yielded "maturity frameworks" for all kinds of different things, from security to privacy, to risk management and mobile device management — the list goes on. I trust you are already familiar with the concept of maturity models — if not, it will be quite useful to look it up. You can do a Web search for "*<insert anything> maturity model*," and you are likely to find a well thought out roadmap, if you will, on how to make any of your solutions or processes more robust. The relevant aspect of maturity for our current discussion is the measurement of the level of "business alignment" and the evaluation of how well we speak our organization's language in terms of deriving and showing benefits and continuous improvement.

Understanding your level of business alignment is a crucial exercise. The SABSA[11] model supports that quite well, and another one, by Jerry Luftman, from 2000 as well.[12]

The concept of "maturity" is often used when we implement or evaluate processes and solutions. But what does it mean? For an entirely non-technical view, let's look at the thesaurus now. Before we go making checklists out of standards and maturity assessments (quite useful though), let's contemplate for a moment, that really, when we talk about a process' maturity, we mean to describe its level of "adulthood" (i.e. its alignment with the organization's goals, and its capability for sustainable functioning in the world as such), its ability to produce outcomes, experience (of the owner or implementer), sophistication, completeness, and I would also add: fitness for its purpose. The CMMI, NIST CSF and other models define their own attributes, though.

With that in mind, let's look at another problematic area. In general, the go-to approach for having a comprehensive view of our security framework, and individual solutions is to use a widely adopted standard. That is, unless you have an excellent grasp of the strategy, risk profile and risk appetite of your company. Because, in that case, standards will not be your starting point — they will be your guides. But let's assume our goal is to "implement ISO27001" — this is not an uncommon goal, even if the reasons are sometimes dubious.

The seemingly obvious part is that you are supposed to implement control measures laid out by the standards, in the way they are described, especially in the case of standards you can be certified or audited against, such as ISO27001 or PCI-DSS.

That kind of approach leads very quickly to blind copying and forcing of standards on the part of the implementer, meaning even, using the very text of the actual standard as a policy. That is quite counterproductive in achieving real results and real compliance even. Forcing the particular way of doing things prescribed by the standards will lead to creating artificial structures in organization, procedures, and reporting, that are alien to the way your company operates. That leads to a problematic introduction, painful operations, and eventually, the body (your organization) rejects the "foreign parts."

The implementation of control measures is the most effective when you look at each requirement as an open question (such as "How do I make XYZ work in this situation?") instead of an answer looking for problems. Starting to look for solutions relevant in your particular case to each point will open up a lot of opportunities for cooperation, shared effort and success, instead of you sitting in your ivory tower making up new restrictions all day long. So, anything written in a standard, framework or other industry publication, is a question, or rather multiple questions. Don't look to figure out the best way to *force* them but figure out how to best embed them in your organization in a *productive* way, using practices that *may already exist* in some way.

Answering these questions when you are met with a new "requirement," you will find out how it currently is or, how it can be, adopted inside your organization and aligned to your situation:

- Why is this particular security measure relevant and important for us? (You must believe it is important, otherwise you will have a tough time convincing others. You may as well find that it isn't so important after all!)

- How does this security measure fit into the big picture (i.e., our organization's strategic goals, services, business structure, financial state, risk profile, risk appetite, our current IT and security framework, architecture, infrastructure and processes)?

- What are the risks we are addressing, and what benefits can we derive from this change? How do we create (or protect) strategic business value? (Don't be disappointed, but "strategic business value" often means the bottom line, or "money".)

- How is the risk or risks, mitigated by this particular control measure, being addressed today in our company? Think not just by the Security Department but across the organization!

- What organizational, procedural, or technical environment or solutions exist today in our company which, with some adjustment, could fulfill this requirement or facilitate the introduction of this security measure?

- Who in my management or lateral organization has a problem or challenge this particular measure (in its entirety, or part of it, or with a bit of tailoring) would help address? Are they in a position to effectively support us in addressing this — for shared benefits? In other words: with whom are we, or can we be, interdependent?13

Aligning the security measures to the organization is much more productive than trying to align the organization to the rules!

Once we start on the path to be perfectly aligned with our organization, why stop there? To illustrate the importance of context, let me walk you through the "chain of security needs," which is analogous with, and follows the supply chain itself. Let's take a simplistic approach to define the supply chain for our purposes. There are the suppliers, your organization in the middle, and then there are your clients or customers.

Are you working for an organization providing goods or services to other companies, or even consumers? Let's get aligned with those customers! Often corporate clients of a service company providing outsourced services will provide a quite comprehensive list of security and control requirements along with their functional needs, and these requirements end up driving that particular company's security in every way. That leads to chaos. That, however, can be prevented and remedied if the security leader takes an inventory of all the different client needs and finds a common set of controls, which will support the development of the company's internal security framework. Better yet, as a service provider, your company can become a security consultant to its clients as well — going ahead of the requirements, educating clients on the particular risks related to services provided by the company.[14]

Ask yourself: if you were your client, and you looked at your company just slightly more than skin deep, would you trust your company?

Let's take this even further! Use client rigor in terms of security and control requirements and transfer that rigor to your suppliers! Banking is a good example here in general as banking laws often prescribe in detail, the requirements for the management of third party risk, and what controls to enforce on your third parties. Usually, it is the same set of requirements that your company itself must fulfill. Also, the organization is directly held liable for whatever damage its outsource partner or vendor causes (or allows to happen). It is, as such, useful to relate all this to the chapter on Sourcing and Suppliers.

Another sensitive matter with great potential for value creation is the problem of new technologies and practices – issues making security people's heads hurt at the time were bring-your-own-device, cloud adoption, or social media. I am sure you can name a few others. If we attempt to prohibit using new technology during the course of business activities, we will risk

losing the potential productivity improvements or other benefits, to be gained by adopting them. To make matters worse,
risks inherent in the use of these technologies will increase
when that use is unregulated and uncontrolled.[15]

Most of the organizations I had the opportunity to work on
security at, the use of privately owned devices, particularly
smartphones, was a real security issue. The problem was that
as technology developed, more and more users "found ways"
to connect their devices to either the corporate network, the
mailing system or both, and more. That was mostly due to human error, some oversight on the part of sysadmins. An option
left unchecked, or a mistake made during a migration that was
never rolled back or fixed – reasons can be endless. The result
was that by the time IT management started to look at "BYOD
strategy," it was already happening in a big way – leaving considerable gaps in security as hundreds or even thousands of unwitting employees were trying to become more productive by
syncing their emails to their personal devices. In some cases
there were traces of restrictive written policies to be found,
only slightly improving the situation as those "more equal"[16] in
the organization would be provided (or allowed to use) the forbidden solution.

So, trying to completely ban a particular technology without
understanding how it works in detail and putting proper controls in place, is most often a futile effort. Also, as there are exceptions in absolutely all situations and to all security
measures, it is crucial, and telling, whether we handle these as

part of our predefined procedures, or we (inadvertently) give the impression of favoritism.

So it is worthwhile to reconsider what those new technologies are, that we have turned a blind eye to — we prohibit them in our policies, but enforcement is lacking? The greatest danger of banning a technology or solution is that then we are unable to define any security measures around it, so anyone still managing to install or use that software, hardware or procedure, most likely uses it with zero protection and control. Also, keep in mind that any single restriction will never provide complete protection against any particular threat.[17]

Also, if you look, should be able to you find some good and working solutions across your organization, which may even have yielded tangible risk reduction or benefit — don't miss the opportunity to roll those out across the board. The working solutions should also be highlighted to management in support of a new addition to your security toolset. It will help to "sell" the new and advanced solution or procedure, just like the ideas in the next chapter.

NOTE SIX
on Selling

"Our best "security" yet, we are very excited about it!"

Do you like Apple products? If so, it may be due to any reason. The important thing is that the company is telling and showing us what to love, in very effective ways. Don't you wish you had such enthusiasm for security in your organization and additional funding and organizational support, to secure your organization, to go with it?

My most current and memorable source of inspiration and the moment when the penny dropped was when I watched "The Wolf of Wall Street" — ethical considerations aside. If "Sell me this pen" doesn't ring a bell, then watch that movie, the clip when the pen is "sold" will bring the idea home. So how can security be sold? In brief, we must show its value and creating the demand — need, or desire — first.

Attention!

First of all, your job is to get noticed! Consider what kind of management forums and communication channels — formal or informal — are available to you besides those you already use. Keep your eyes open for relevant and successful business strategies and news of high profile security breaches in the world — and share these with your management, adding your own narrative! Let's look at how professional marketers and salespeople do it, using the AIDA model[18] and borrow some of those tactics.

Like it or not, selling is a significant and vital part of the security job. Even when the value of a security solution is well understood within our organization — which is quite often not the case as we have seen — you still haven't succeeded. You are just getting noticed. At this point, you can present your proposals for action. At this point, you simply "leveled up," meaning now you are competing with business initiatives and opportunities for funding. If our initiatives are considered alongside all other proposed actions, we have created a good foundation for further efforts to secure the organization. Let's not forget, from our point of view, being able to play at that level is a great achievement compared to just being a line item in the IT budget.

Most of the time, fear tactics are used to convince management of the need for security spending. That is quite unfortunate as we are selling ourselves short, possibly talking to the

wrong crowd (not decision-makers) and creating or reinforcing the already negative connotations for security. How about
we strike a more positive note, and beside loss avoidance, we
emphasize the added benefits of our current and proposed activities, such as potentially increasing flexibility and even efficiency for the whole organization.

So is that what we are selling? Yes, we are selling the benefits
of good security, no more, no less, so our job is to show those
benefits and business value. You don't have to be revolutionary
or even original. However, it is essential to find whom to sell
to! If you are a door-to-door salesman, selling anything related
to the fundamental infrastructure of that house, going from
house to house, you will want to talk to the owner of the house.
You can sell to an owner but not to a tenant of a rental prop-
erty. Similarly, if you engage people who are not decision-makers for discovering and shaping the prevailing opinion and behavior, but someone who does not have the authority, they will
not be in a position to "buy" what you are selling. If that happens, you will get stuck in a place where no real conversations
with real decision-makers can happen. Not good. If you are a
consultant, then you make no sale. If you are inside an organization, you make no progress.

On the other hand, having an ear for the challenges of each
part of your organization — especially outside of the IT do-
main — will yield very useful information. That will not only
help shaping your message for decision-makers but may actu-

ally indicate an issue which can be solved or alleviated by a particular security initiative — improving the conditions across the organization.

Interest

Even if issues are recognized, there can be a multitude of options to go about any particular challenge, and "doing nothing" is always a tempting one as it may cost nothing today — but it yields nothing in the future, either, or may even end up costing the company dearly! That is where selling comes into play to challenge the status quo.

With regards to incoming "demand" for security, us, security guys are in a particularly difficult position, compared to "delivery" type departments, such as legacy IT development and service delivery. They are mostly "asked" to deliver. Security people are rarely "asked" to deliver a strategy to fight advanced persistent threats,[19] deploy next-generation network security or awareness training — if not in the wake of a major breach or incident. More often than not, we must put effort into showing and explaining what our services are and what kind of problems – risks – they are capable of addressing. We have to know what we can and must do, share this information with our internal customers in a way that makes sense to them, and leads to recognition of the need and eventually to "wanting" security.

Desire

So, you need a sales pitch. Selling is the easiest when demand already exists. Many get discouraged when it doesn't. However, the fact is, for security, it seldom exists readily, so we must either create it or dig deeper to find it.

Turning "I like it" to "I want it" is the key in all of this.[20] Money talks. What can make top management want security? Most often it is an external driver, such as a regulatory mandate or a set of client requirements, or, sometimes a belated reaction to a breach. In such cases, it is not too difficult to obtain sponsorship, but still, take all the steps in this chapter! What if no such mandates exist in your industry or business, yet, common sense would dictate a certain level of security — and you feel you are doing less than that. Not improving (or rather, not spending money on improving) protection may be a sound business decision in some cases. A well-executed risk assessment can identify areas where that is the case, versus those, where improvement is needed to protect or improve the bottom line.

Here is one example of how security helped save a large sum of money for one particular company. In brief, they were experiencing network bandwidth limitations and were about to upgrade their network. It turned out that there was an undiscovered or unhandled malware infection across the network, causing an exponential increase in network traffic. With the malware eventually eradicated, the company did not need to pay for any additional bandwidth.

Another great example of such dynamic was the introduction of bankcards equipped with a chip, based on the EMV standard.[21] This technology allows more advanced protection of payment data on the card as the chip would replace the magnetic stripe as the primary storage medium for authentication information. In the meantime, contactless payments, as the next generation of point of sale payments, are becoming mainstream but still the story has its lessons for us.

What happened was the following. Adopting the chip-based standard meant additional high costs for financial institutions issuing payment cards. At the same time, the chip was often viewed as just another compliance requirement, a security measure which, of course, reduces risk but, even with losses from card fraud compensations included, apparently costs of the implementation would outweigh the level of risk reduction. There was, however, a deadline set by the body governing payment card security and card brands themselves also. Not adopting the chip by that particular deadline would mean that the financial institution had had to seize issuing cards of those popular brands. Eventually, of course, all financial institutions wanting to issue those particular brands adopted this new technology. But the lesson is in what happened before that deadline.

Besides enhancing security, chips embedded on the cards provide numerous additional opportunities – for marketing. Among other uses, chips on payment cards enable new ways of supporting loyalty programs by storing credits (points) accrued on the payment card itself. Banks can partner with merchants or service providers in jointly issuing cards – they can reward shoppers for using the card in particular ways.

As this arrangement is primarily realized by information technology, the IT and security department would play an essential role in its successful adoption and implementation. That being the case, if representatives of those areas recognized the benefits and proactively supported the adoption of chip cards, then they could enable their companies to gain substantial business advantage by speeding up the process of adoption. Especially, as in this case also, being the first, or at least being among the first ones is essential. In mid-2008 only 34 percent of payment cards were equipped with a chip.[22] By 2011, due to sanctions put forward by card companies, almost all cards issued had a chip on them. Nevertheless, in 2010, loyalty applications were still only adopted by the most progressive banks; they were able to realize additional business benefits then and are still enjoying and building on those today.

We must recognize that it is often the security department who either blocks or at least makes it far more difficult to adopt such new technologies than it should be. That occurs either by assigning disproportionately high risks to it and so in effect falsely alarming management, or annoying everyone by proposing overly complicated and restrictive security policies and rigorous controls.

However, in this situation, security can drive competitive advantage by enabling (vs. blocking) the fast and secure business adoption of new technologies. That can be achieved by acting fast in the right direction, adjusting our policies and procedures, or creating new ones, appropriate for the latest technology, allowing the business to utilize it in a controlled manner, instead of trying to ban it.[23]

Action

Rather: constant action. Creating momentum by keeping an operating and reporting rhythm and tackling low hanging fruits can be quite straightforward. Quick wins, however trivial, will create the setup for moving to more comprehensive solutions.

Following up with your boss and stakeholders is critical. Mostly this will be a "push" type of communication, instead of a "pull." That means it is up to you to insist on, prepare for, deliver, and follow-up on decisions on your one-to-one or security council/board meetings. Your primary stakeholders often struggle to find time for you — sometimes though, particularly when a high-profile cyberattack hits the news, they come to you. Even though in recent years there has been some interest in security in boardrooms with massive data breaches making headlines and concerns for privacy on the rise, still, we must raise the awareness, interest, and engagement for this topic. It does not happen automatically. *One of the biggest lessons I learned in the area of visibility is that "no news" is not "good news,"* in terms of stakeholder interaction. Some of us, including myself, are sometimes happy to be left alone with our teams to do our jobs. But if that leads to stakeholders becoming out of touch with security risks, and us becoming out of touch with business priorities than that disconnect will alienate us from the core of our organization. It is quite easy to fall victim of not only external threats but also internal obstacles too, such as company politics or financial planning procedures. Not being "bothered" all the time may feel nice on the surface. You may think that everyone is clear on your priorities, and the great job you and your team are doing is appreciated. If there is nothing wrong, there is no reason to talk about anything. Right?

That is, however, a dangerous and immature attitude and will backfire over time. Neglecting communication and withholding information showing your and your team's constant progress toward agreed goals, objectives, and targets *will not create, much less reinforce the perception that you are doing a great job*, and everything is fine. It will eventually cause your management to consider a lot of things, like if the budget and/or headcount of the security department could be reduced, or if you really are the right person for the job of security manager or CISO?

It is in the nature of what we do that we must continuously push our agenda, even harder than different business departments, and in that struggle, we are handicapped as we seldom produce tangible business value or hard profit. At least it's not apparent — and that is precisely why it is vital to show our results against risk and security metrics agreed with management.

In many of the organizations I worked for, the management forums for security were almost entirely disconnected from business activities. The agenda is generally put together by the security manager, and the level of interest of management and business relevance of topics discussed directly shows the level of understanding of the business or organizational goals by the security manager. It is often not a pretty picture as discussions are heavy on compliance and light on business risk. Also, if this is a one-way exchange, that's bad. We need questions, problems, concerns from the business side. However, for that, we must be able to connect what we do with what the business does. Even better, define what we do, based on business goals!

Often business leaders need *your* help in grasping the adverse effects of insufficient security measures, and the positive ones of those that operate effectively. Just as we need to have the support of the masses, we cannot do without the senior management being on board. Also, there is a very particular mindset those experienced people have — that of an investor.

on Being an Investor

"... and the need for a broader mindset"

THE PURCHASE OF ANYTHING IS AN INVESTMENT in its perceived usefulness, whether we order the newest gadget from the Web or fund a security project. Smart investors have a very particular mindset that allows for prudent investment. The perception of anything we purchase is shaped by clever sales techniques and our own research, and even though we were discussing selling techniques earlier, all of that must be based on valid research and presented as such. That is why we, security professionals, need to care about what investors think. So what kind of investors are we talking about here?

Are You an Investor?

To understand how top management judges the benefits of any activity, you must adopt the mindset of an investor. Become an investor yourself — in your area of expertise: technology and security in our case. You have the advantage of knowing the field, having an understanding of technology and trends deeper than the "average" investor, who will rely on analyst reports and the opinions of others. That will help to form your own opinion. That is essential because according to the world's greatest investors, the key to successful investing – as to anything else in my opinion as well – is to rely on your own judgment, after due research, making up your own mind about things!

Buying some well-researched stocks, you think have great future potential, will provide you with a new and handy angle for keeping an eye on the trends in your industry, making you, in turn, a better professional as well! It's a beautiful effect, which works both ways, since the two 'sides' are reinforcing and feeding each other! You don't need to invest vast amounts of your resources. Smaller amounts work just as well to increase your incentives for keeping a keen interest in where the world is heading.

Trends and Earnings Calls

Look a bit wider in the technology space. What are the current major trends? Such trends and major shifts happening in the late 2010's and early 2020's were, for example:

- The big data concept is starting to be realized by technologies like Hadoop, which is an open-source project of the Apache Software Foundation.

- The wearables market is just coming alive with smart bands and watches being put out – Apple, for example, has recently introduced the Apple Watch.
- Cloud SaaS started to boom with a stable outlook, exemplified by Salesforce, Shopify, and ServiceNow. Cloud PaaS is becoming mainstream, spearheaded by Microsoft, Amazon, and Google.
- At the core of all cloud are virtualization and containerization. Look at VMware.
- Blockchain is at the top of the hype, all the big tech companies are invested in it, but real practical applications are yet to be seen, aside from cryptocurrencies.

After identifying your top interests in terms of trends and companies, do your research on them. There is quite an extensive literature on this topic. I will only highlight one particularly useful resource here: the quarterly earnings calls. You may think that the discussion on these occasions is strictly limited to financial metrics like revenue, margin or profit and loss ratio. Of course, a lot of the information shared is of such nature. But guess what? A significant portion of these calls is spent with discussing the company's vision; what the particular company is up to in the next quarters, in terms of their business activities, new products and services, top projects, directions. That is where, being in touch with the significant companies this way has a triple advantage for us — both the security professional and the investor in you, gets information. The great news is that on these earnings calls, in addition to financial data, that investors are interested in, you will gain valuable information on where the industry is headed, what the major trends are. All that, already digested and spoon-fed to you by the top executives in the industry! It's like a free webinar, and even better.

Next to sharing financial results and future technology (market) outlook, these calls are also sales pitches — just not to customers, but investors. You[24] will receive the highlights of the company's last quarter (or year, depending on what time of the financial year you are at) and also the future outlook with regards to their key products, services, and strategic plans. Listen to what CEOs and CFOs say here, and how they are saying it, what information they share and what they keep to themselves. *People talking on the earnings calls are in the same kinds of positions as those leading your company as well, so it's useful to know what they talk about and how they do that.*

Due Diligence

Your top management will evaluate your proposed solutions for improving security, just like you would value a company before buying its stock (and while owning it) — that is called due diligence. Basic due diligence questions, such as the following, should be asked. Think of your solution as a candidate in Shark Tank[25] — and adapt the questions to evaluate your security program and solutions!

- What is the leader like? Can I trust that person?
- What is the company selling? How proprietary/useful is it?
- How big is the market for it?
- What is the track record of the company?
- What is the outlook in terms of growth?
- Does their activity make sense for you, based on your experience? Do they follow trends, or go against them, or are they ahead of the market somehow?
- What kind of earnings and margin ratios do they have?
- Is the company making or losing money?

All that is about broadening your horizons: once you have adopted the investor's mindset, it will make much more sense and be quite straightforward for you to think in terms of business benefit, profit and loss — and make the business case for security.

NOTE EIGHT
on Finance

"How not to actually have zero budget"

BUSINESS SCHOOL IS NOT THE FIRST CHOICE of security profession-als. However, everyone in any management position must deal with finances. Money does not only make the world go around, but it is also our most fundamental resource — assuming, of course, that you are successful in your selling efforts and your initiatives get funded. If not, you will *actually* have zero budget!

Ensuring we can spend that money is also something we must take care of ourselves; the allocation and control of the appropriate budget for security, according to the rules of the company, is an essential part of securing the organization. Se-curity industry surveys have been forecasting a constant in-crease in security budgets — but that won't happen by itself.

Don't think of money of as your only resource, far from it! Still, financial planning as part of strategic planning is essential; it is also necessary to relate the security budget goals (along with the security strategy itself) to business priorities. So, let's look at how we do that, on a very general and high level.

How much does Security cost?

It is quite problematic to figure out how much an organization *really* spends on security. That is because actual security spending will not only consist of the CISO's budget line items, like security related salaries, security tools and services. The security spending category also includes budget items not directly controlled by the CISO, but still contributing to the level of protection — and we must be cognizant of those expenditures as well.

Different types of expenses are allocated to different parts of the organization in each company. At one organization, you will see the security department or office controlling all costs that can be related to security. In other companies, it may be the IT operations department which controls expenses associated with all running information systems, be it telephony, or even security, as long as it has already been "annualized." Like for instance, running license and support costs of endpoint protection software. At one particular company, the license cost of the antivirus package (as it was called at the time) was borne by security and the support cost was taken by IT operations. That required additional logistics within the organization, counteracting clarity. Some companies are preoccupied with the accounting magic of CAPEX vs. OPEX, favoring one versus the other at different stages of their organizational maturity and development, depending on decisions of the CFO and the board.

A security leader will likely not get very far without understanding his or her, and to the extent possible, other IT and even surrounding departments' budget structures (that comes in to play in your chargeback efforts). Figure out what types of expenses are recognized according to what specific rules, the organization's strategies and preferences for cost and resource allocation,[26] what kinds of costs fall within your budget, do you have your own budget for security with authority to spend it, and just as importantly, according to what schedule the annual financial planning is done.

Dress for success

The schedule is an integral part of, and the annual budgeting cycle has an immense effect on the execution and even the definition of the security strategy. Practically all organizations operate according to some strategic, operational, and financial plan. Strategic plans are created for several years ahead, but each year an annual plan is drawn up to address changes and to define as much detail as possible to allow execution of those plans. In line with this yearly planning cycle, usually towards the end of each summer, the annual budgeting cycle starts. Annual budgets include, among many other things, the amounts of money foreseen to be spent the following year. Your budget will stay with you for at least the next year; any exceptional spending is likely to be difficult if not impossible, depending on your company's policy. There should always be emergency funds available, but don't spend those on things you can plan for in advance.

This method of operations will impose a quite strict limitation during the year as it is not possible to exert the same level of influence over our budget during other times of the year, as during the planning cycle. We must work for our lunch during the annual planning cycle and beyond.

To make things worse, it's impossible to come too early to this party. Considering what you will need next year during the summer may sound early enough. It isn't. If you think about what you need next year only when you receive the annual planning spreadsheets from the finance department, you are very, very late. You may not realize that until your well-thought-out new security line items disappear from the planned budget during consecutive planning rounds. They disappear because they mean nothing to no one.

So when should you think about future items? All elements of your security program should be on your mind all the time but reviewed at least monthly. Also, constant internal marketing efforts are needed. As a result of conscious planning, each major security initiative should have been pitched to any and preferably all decision making authorities in your organization at least once by spring, for security budget items to have any chance of surviving the lawnmower effect of the budgeting rounds during the fall. The best approach would be:

- "selling" all year

- getting generic high-level endorsement for the security strategy itself, then
- explain each security initiative using, if possible, targeted sessions, get key stakeholders on board, then
- obtain formal approval of individual initiatives/work packages with their costs and benefits included, separately from the consolidated budget.

All this should happen, aligned with the financial planning schedules of your company; some activities well before the official planning cycle, some during it. But beware. Whatever marketing and communication steps are left to do during the fall planning cycle will inevitably suffer in the rush of the planning process itself across the organization and the pitching and discussions of all the other investments anyone else in your company is looking to get funded. All that is made more difficult with deadlines for completing each phase of the annual planning. You can't convince everyone within a few weeks.

Individual initiatives are best presented using the format of a business case. Some organizations mandate submitting any form of budget request in a fixed business case template but be aware that decision-makers will ultimately weigh your proposed budget items against all others, which include all those elements actually driving profits or directly supporting the business. Security is at a handicap as showing benefits is a challenge. If you are not speaking the language and following the structure of business cases either, showing technical details of the threat du jour and architectural drawings of the proposed solution to decision-makers, that handicap becomes an insurmountable barrier.

Business cases usually contain, among other information, details of the financial impact of the proposal, considering direct and indirect costs, and the total cost of ownership (TCO). At the stage where you are just getting your stakeholders on board to support the initiative when it comes to approvals, it is quite okay to use estimations for showing costs and benefits.

At the time of approval though, an initial sourcing effort should have already been completed, and a detailed breakdown of financial costs and benefits is needed. That is represented in the form of a financial impact statement (FIS) or similar type of document. This document usually is in tabular format, detailing costs and benefits in a tabular format, broken down to the type of cost and represented on a quarterly or monthly basis. It is best to work with a monthly base and aggregate to quarterly summary when presenting.

Financial planning schedules

The activities described above are quite important, but still, it is not always strictly enforced by the organization, many times it is up to anyone interested in securing a budget, to justify it in the best way possible beforehand. The actual budgeting process is driven by your finance department, according to an annual recurring schedule which they publish. At that time, multiple budgeting rounds can follow over the course of several months even, starting from late August to around October each year. Your initial submission will be rolled up together with all other plans, scrutinized, and weighed against each other. That is when your preparatory sales work can pay off. Familiar security items with well-understood justifications are less likely to get removed from the plan. Whereas some line item with an esoteric technical name such as "web application firewall," costing six figures annually and bringing most likely little direct profit, unclear, or intangible benefits is an easy target for budget cuts.

After all this struggle, you will be quite happy to see some of your new budget items kept in the final approved budget around December. Then, you must likely wait until several months into the following year, to be able to spend it.

Budget structure

Propagated in massive spreadsheets or using an enterprise resource planning software, budgets are generally very well structured, according to the organization's accounting set up, as they address the whole organization. It will take some effort to acquaint yourself with those. The first time around, it is best to ask for help from the department that created it, to best understand what is what. There will be separate places for your one time, and recurring costs, capital, and operating expenditures, and each type of charge, like human resources, hardware, or licenses, are also separated. If however, your budget request submission is lacking in content, or not following the structure or logic prescribed, you will be asked to rework it, if you are lucky. Worst case, your erroneous submission may be processed as is, and you only find out later that you are not getting any of the funding you hoped for. Remember; still, no one is babysitting you!

Spending the money

Just like obtaining funds as part of our budget, while spending money, you must also follow company rules. First, the funds are not available immediately after approval. Usually, funds defined in the budget are released around March.

So, March is when actual payments can likely start, so any recurring monthly fees, especially for services beginning that January, will probably be paid with some form of exception -- unless there is a procedure to cover new or standing recurring costs. Anything you pay for needs to go through a successful tendering process as well. We will talk about purchasing security equipment and services later. Once however — in generic terms again — the purchasing, contracting and at least the first scheduled delivery is completed, the buying organization confirms delivery/completion. Then the vendor issues their invoice and based on that, the funds allocated to the particular item can be paid.

Chargeback

A working system of allocating and charging ICT costs to the business is an indication of a mature organization. Often though, it is the supporting departments with long service history and more tangible services that can do a full and structured chargeback. An example of a service routinely allocated and charged to business units are facilities. It is pretty straightforward to calculate occupied space according to the number of people in a particular department. That is quite an oversimplification, but you get the idea.

ICT services, however, have not had such a history of cost allocation, and creating a fair allocation scheme is quite challenging as usage data is often not readily available in sufficient detail. When it comes to security services, the challenge is even more significant, and rarely seen.

- Anything provided by the security department is not defined as a service, and so the necessary parameters for measurement are missing;
- Setting up a fair allocation scheme is just as tough as with generic ICT services;
- Some security services are easy to relate to individual employees, like identity management or endpoint protection,

others, however, serve a frequently changing set of users, or not even getting in contact with the business directly, but only through the IT organization, like vulnerability management. Those need to be charged back to the IT department (who would, in turn, bake all that into their costs, which can be then allocated to end-users).

- The chargeback of security services can only be as good as the ICT or other chargeback arrangements within the organization.

- Never go into chargeback arrangements without an excellent grasp of the risk profile and priorities of your company; otherwise, your costs, seemingly disconnected from business goals, will be rejected. Over-complicating your chargeback scheme will not be helpful either, as it can become an administrative nightmare; you being stuck just focusing on and justifying costs. Without context that is destined to fail.

I often wonder: if attackers need to spend less and less on attack capabilities,[27] and the costs of breaches to us are steadily increasing,[28] how long are we expecting to get away with allocating disproportionately little on protection?

PHASE THREE

TRANSFORM

NOTE NINE
on Being Effective

"Simplify and focus"

THE MASSIVE WAVES IN THE OCEAN are created by a large number of tiny streams, all pushing in the same direction. If there were no direction of these small streams, the big wave would never be formed. The same way, all of our actions need to be directed toward a common goal to be impactful, let's call that strategy or long-term plan. To realize your plan, you need to make an impact by *simplifying your communication, distinguishing activity from achievement, and targeted communication and action* (i. e. delivering just one message at a time and keeping your strategy to yourself when sharing it doesn't drive the discussion forward).

Simplify

We strive to manage the vast complexity of a corporate information security program and the diversity of threats and protection measures as they are when our job is to understand, make sense of, and simplify all that. Simplification is such a fundamental principle we often still forget about it or shy away from it, to avoid making people think we "are" simple. The fact is, the more mature a leader is, the more "simple" things are, fundamentally, they either support or hinder the achievement of business goals.

We also often increase the complexity of our security architecture ourselves, by being busy implementing more and more stuff. That is not sustainable, so your top priority should be first to use what you have to its full potential, be it a security appliance or procedure. Only after taking stock of our current capabilities should we consider planning for a new addition. After all, we need to spend less and less and still achieve more and more. It doesn't help to overthink and over-design things.

However, simplification of the multifaceted issues security professionals face, and connecting them to organizational priorities in a relevant way needs considerable thought. Spending some time thinking about how all of our activities will make sense and become achievements is an absolute necessity to identify the steps that will make the most significant positive impact.

Once, as a junior consultant, I was involved in a security risk assessment, that went on for months, and was very detailed and structured. We interviewed a lot of people, analyzed threats to all the several hundred types of assets, used a multitude of complicated spreadsheets. Our methodology must have been world class. At the end though, when presenting our results to the management, they looked at it, perplexed, and the CEO asked: 'Guys, how come that the most critical system is the one we use to book meeting rooms with?'

It wasn't. It could have been, but no. *Whatever methodology you use for assessing risk, it should include ways to ensure that the end result makes business sense.*

Activity vs. Achievement

Establishing norms and baselines is a challenging activity, mainly due to psychological reasons. It is very tempting, to allow ourselves to get lost in the diverse multitude of exceptions and try addressing them on a case by case basis. Exceptions are many times manifested by events or incidents requiring urgent attention. Dealing with these gives us an instant a sense of purpose, the feeling of achievement in the short term. We feel like we are contributing.

But however productive one may feel in such situations; the reality is the very opposite, that is when we are going nowhere really fast. Don't confuse activity with achievement.

Realizing we are stuck in this vicious cycle is difficult. It is mainly so because it doesn't even occur to someone trapped in this situation. However, once you recognize your predicament, you can move past it.

If you want to establish baselines and norms, don't stay preoccupied with the exceptions. After realizing that you are swamped with addressing different anomalies, you can make a conscious decision to ignore them temporarily. Obviously, in a security professional's life, there are always some legitimately pressing matters — completely ignoring them is not the prudent course of action, for sure. Still, find ways to shift your focus to where you want to be in the future, rather than where you are now. To see where you need to be going with your security program, try to ignore the noise created by outlier cases. Take a good look at where the priorities and the majority of the pain points are, and what the state you want to achieve is.

Simplification also means reducing the number of exceptions. To be able to define exceptions, first you need to set the norms against which those exceptions can be raised (or, exist already, perhaps without us being cognizant of them). If we have no standards, then everything will necessarily be handled at as an exception, because then, each case requires 'special' attention and individual case-by-case decisions. That means we effectively deal with 100% of all cases individually, which is very far from sustainable. Rolling out a well-defined baseline will result in around 70% of the cases (instances, systems) to fall within the norm, and leave only the rest, as exceptions. That, in turn, will allow us to concentrate our limited resources and attention on the much smaller number of 'outliers' (i.e., the 30% worth of exceptions), and effectively forget about the 'normal' 70% which may trigger a small incident but still conforms to our norms.

The outlier 30% will also be useful as signals to detect undesirable events and trends and show areas for improvement.

After clarifying your mission for yourself, go step by step, literally! Again, do not expect anyone to be interested in frameworks and other abstract stuff. Do communicate vision, expected results, and benefits, but give one message at a time. That may mean one focus action monthly or even quarterly — that's it, no more! Also, by the way, that is not a cause for frustration, that is just the way it is.

One at a Time

Instead of painting the big picture time and time again, only convey one message at a time. I started experimenting with presentation techniques like Steve Jobs when he says: 'I have three things for you today.' Even that may be too much for your purposes. My experience shows that everyone's happier, including you and your audience, if you say: 'I've got one key thing for you today.' It's a tough assignment but never fall into the trap of writing a long letter because you have no time to write a short one.[29] A few sentences about how the current topic fits into the big picture doesn't hurt. However, it's no use going into details and elaborating on the background over and over again. Besides, keeping it brief will tell the decision-makers that you respect their time, which is their most precious asset. They will appreciate that.

Focusing your limited resources on achieving one goal (or a minimal set of goals) at a time, makes all the difference. Just like Lord Nelson at Trafalgar: destroying enemy ships one at a time, with all of his vessels engaging that single ship. One new thing at a time may mean one focused topic each month or even each quarter. That's all, no more!

What's more memorable: a person talking about something different each day, or someone who has one single topic, or even slogan, and he keeps repeating it every day?

I also recommend that you gain an understanding of your stakeholders' main priorities. Put yourself in their shoes. They may fundamentally agree with what you are proposing; only the timing is inopportune. I suggest you have a strategy, but keep it to yourself. Don't expect anyone else to be on board with everything by default.

Have a strategy but keep it to yourself

Everyone's busy. I've tried many times to show fancy diagrams and complex frameworks to explain everything and show management that I have a vision, structure, and strategy for security. However, while I was going through all that, everyone was losing interest, and by the time I got to the points of action, there weren't any ears open anymore. The funny thing is that I tried to start from square one each time, trying to put things into context, because I realized how busy everyone was. That approach may be useful for didactic purposes, but it won't help move things forward. IT managers want to know what is required of them from a security perspective without too much background — until they feel their operations are not disturbed too much. The why usually needs to be discussed separately from the what and the how. Show why a particular security measure is relevant to the business, but if you want action, talk about what and how, and not something else. By that something else I mean the extra security strategy and roadmap and all your telling a little story. That takes attention away from the actual tasks at hand. So, try this: *have a strategy for the big picture but avoid discussing it unless it's pertinent to the discussion at hand.* Keep it to yourself and each time focus on just one part of it, with which you want to move forward. Don't expect others to fully understand the complexity and importance of a comprehensive security framework and such esoteric things. That, and translating it into action is your job. Do not expect others to put 'your' priorities in front of their own. After you clarify main priorities with the key stakeholders, share with others, and take the steps — one by one. Sometimes these steps need to be baby steps.

NOTE TEN
on Processes

"How will everyone know how to contribute?"

DO YOU LIKE ASKING THE SAME QUESTIONS to the same people regularly? Do you enjoy asking the same "favors" all the time? Do you like people who do that to you? Have you ever considered why those things may happen? We are so used to the chaotic and information-overloaded way we operate today; we don't even stop to figure out whether there are some ways we can alleviate that pressure. For security-related activities to go smoothly and be manifested as an integral part of the organization's daily practices, it is essential to discover or create the connections between the two.

Policies are Static — Processes are Dynamic

Producing static lists of requirements in the form of policy type documents is insufficient to achieve any level of integration with real life and deliver results. The next step in producing a practical security framework is going beyond describing "what" should be done, by specifying "who" should perform whatever is defined by the policy, and "how" that needs to happen. According to widely adopted practice, that is best done by defining processes — or redefining, amending, tweaking, existing ones. In any case, the expected flow of events and actions, along with their triggers, inputs, outputs, and organizational roles responsible for executing those actions, need to be agreed and formalized (written down in a structured manner). Often that distinction between the policies defining "what" and processes determining "how," is absent. That leaves an information vacuum in terms of the interpretation of the security policies in real life. As an example, ITIL makes no real distinction between "functions" and "processes." Discussing that in detail is beyond the scope of this book. Suffice to say that creating your processes covering all main ITIL areas, is quite challenging. ITIL, however, offers a useful definition of what a process is.[30]

For any policy goal to be achieved or activity to be performed with consistency, you need to have people in your organization who act as owners who, besides defining the process, monitor results as well. Who should own these processes? Many areas we are concerned with are actually "owned" (or should be) by other departments. These are departments, such as those responsible for human resources, legal, facilities management, asset management, purchasing and vendor management, marketing or public relations and, to be sure, for operations of our IT. Our policy defines requirements that pertain to those areas, so it will make sense to place our control measures right into their pre-existing processes. Alternatively, help them create those processes needed for the minimal level of control. Where no other parties exist inside the organization cover functions related to a security measure, you need to own it, define and introduce the process.

Whatever well-known framework's elements you are adopting, the most fruitful approach, again — also the hardest — is to try and embed security measures into procedures of all the areas responsible for actually implementing those measures or following those rules.

This approach is radically different from creating our detailed security policy with great care, declaring that it is mandatory for all – and watch it be ignored during daily operations. It is a bit more difficult to persuade other parts of our organization to allow us to amend their policies and procedures, but it brings great rewards and if done well, can bring benefits to all involved parties.

Defining roles and responsibilities is an essential governance function, and the "process-based" approach has several key elements that make it so useful.

Defining an organizational structure is an essential element of managing any larger entity, and hence a must. The flow of activities, however, frequently span more than one department, and if defined with proper care, represent the operation of our organization in a more useful way than the "organization based" approach. Processes are the conveyor belt between the individual wheels — the departments.

Taking the time to define activities on an "overlay" above departments, ideally in an end-to-end fashion,[31] will prevent many internal operational issues, and each party will know their role in providing results (better security, in our case). Also, the inputs and outputs of each process step and the process itself will create the all-important links to other parts of the organization.

Own or Be Pwned

To adequately define a process, in my experience, at least the following main attributes need to be defined.

Overall purpose, goals, and outcomes of the process

Without an overarching purpose statement, it will be challenging to devise a process that fulfills our needs. Moreover, good performance, after the process is implemented, is almost impossible if those involved in executing the process do not have the purpose and benefits of following the steps of the process at heart. The goals of the process should be defined using the SMART philosophy, mainly to identify metrics (or key performance indicators, KPIs) to monitor the efficiency and effectiveness of execution.

Process flow and process description

The distinct steps of the process need to be separated and defined in detail. The steps of the process are the core entities within a process, and all other attributes are tied to them. No steps — no process.

Roles and responsibilities

There will be multiple roles Responsible for the actual execution — ideally, however, a single role should be Accountable. Accountability for results should lie with a single role or individual; typically, with a management role. Often, after a set of processes are defined as part of a project, they fall into oblivion in the lack of a named accountable owner. The owner can function best if he/she is delegated the necessary authority to drive actions forward, so best allocated to the person Accountable for the process results. The accountable person may delegate the day-to-day coordination responsibility to ensure things move forward, accountability, or final ownership, however, cannot be transferred. Our choice here is *Own or be pwned.*[32] Having no ownership for security and other processes will lead to them becoming defunct. Also, some parties need to be Consulted as part of executing the step, and some may need to be Informed. All of this is best defined in a RACI matrix.[33]

Triggers

Some event-based (or event-triggered) process definition

methods include an entity called "trigger." A trigger is an event, or a defined (and discernible) state of something, which necessitates or invokes a particular activity. Distinguishing the trigger for a specific action to occur can be quite useful, particularly in very complex environments. True, this is one more box on the flowchart in front of each step, but the triggers make understanding why, and in what circumstances a particular activity shall happen adds a lot to the clarity for those involved. A process definition can be created without formal triggers. Using them is a decision to be made, and they should be applied across all processes consistently if we opt for using them.

Inputs

Most activities require some kind of input. A trigger may be one kind of input, but mostly inputs are defined as particular sets of information, documents to be processed, such as the data in a request made by someone in the organization (the event of the claim itself being the trigger). Here we define our information needs for the activity with the highest possible accuracy and detail — ideally in the form of a "form," with "fields."

Outputs

Same as inputs, activities have outputs. If an action has no distinct output, it should not be defined as a separate process step.

Supporting resources

The resources needed to perform the activity should be defined. These include IT systems, and any non-technical elements supporting the activity. By the way, if these are defined adequately, compiling your information asset inventory and plan for business continuity will be quite easy!

Control points (approvals, checks)

A control point or check is one or more distinct steps in a process, where activities required to ensure that the process is executed according to our needs and definitions, are performed. These are typically approvals, validation checks, and other activities representing the four-eye-principle. Not the least, control points should generate evidence of adequate operations to ensure transparency, accountability, and auditability.[34]

Performance indicators

Performance indicators or KPIs are our goals represented by numbers. Having a target (or multiple targets) and measuring against those periodically over time will reflect how our process performs. We can establish lead indicators to measure the effectiveness of our own efforts, and lag indicators to measure the outcomes and results of our activities. A process can have multiple KPIs, representing several goals.

Templates

In a world dominated by paper-based forms, this was a must; we could not operate without well-made forms. More recently, however, if a set of activities is not supported by an IT system, we tend to ignore the utility of pre-structuring our information needs. An IT system cannot be defined without forms, but when there is no IT system, we forego pre-structuring our inputs and outputs. However, we have much to gain with the improvement in efficiency when we do not need to rethink, iterate and validate the information we exchange with those responsible for performing another part of a process — because we have pre-structured our communication.

Multiplying by Division

The coach in a soccer (or any) game can't score a goal. Goals are scored where the ball is. Similarly, the security officer can hardly produce any result in terms of information security by themselves. There are a lot of people in a lot of roles where protection measures can and should be manifested. The best results can be achieved by delegating to where the "security ball" is to drive results — to business and IT organizations, and by utilizing the work of others to oversee those results, such as the internal and external auditors. Internal delegation is mostly two-fold: in a horizontal approach, responsibility for security controls is best allocated to the owners of the business and IT processes, or those involved in those processes daily — process owners and control owners. Vertically into the organization, the department heads should bear responsibility for keeping secure; then, in turn, they should appoint security "champions," who can effectively drive the security mindset further down into the organization. Your job here is twofold. First, you must ensure that the reasons and background for protection efforts are understood and rules and behavior patterns accepted by everyone involved. Second, you must facilitate the delegation process by formalizing rules and creating the framework for your process owners, control owners, and champions to operate in.

The process-based view of your IT and the rest of your organization broadens your horizons and can support the perspective you need to operate effectively. It facilitates finding where security fits into the organization so that it can work in harmony with the rest of the company. That will make all the difference in successfully adopting devops practices as well.

NOTE ELEVEN

on Marketing and Communication

"The best time to talk about security is — all the time!"

It is commonplace that people are the weakest link in the security chain, yet security investments hardly focus on reinforcing it. The Verizon and Ponemon data breach studies cited earlier show that almost half of all reported data breaches can be traced back to human error or misuse. Further analysis of the metadata of those studies shows that in more than eighty percent of those, the root causes of them were inadvertent.[35] My personal experience also shows that even with frequent phishing simulations,[36] the "success rate" of such attacks can't be pushed to below 20%.[37] What can we do? We can do *marketing*.

The origins of the term "marketing" go back to the times when practically 100% of the goods and services sold and bought was tangible, retailed at "markets." Think the likes of farmers, fishers and artisans selling their produce, wares, and labor, hundreds and thousands of years ago. That was fundamentally a seller's market; satisfying customers' needs directly. Overproduction was not an issue; it could not have been either, as mass production had not been invented yet. That environment changed radically during the industrial revolution. Technical and procedural innovations enabled more efficient manufacturing, allowing mass production and led to the formation of glut. The challenge of selling surplus goods then drove producers to figure out new ways of driving sales, developing in essence, marketing, as a profession.

We can go about all that security awareness stuff a bit differently too, by taking a broader approach. Do this:

- Identify your audience and relate to them
- Start with the basics but don't stop there
- Spark interest and engage them
- Keep at it

Here is why and how to do it.

Identify Your Audience and Relate to Them

Wasting our energy talking to everyone about all issues is not practical, and it is not our goal either. The key to effectively spreading the word without damaging our reputation or our relationships with our peers, leaders, and even the general employee population is selectiveness. *Always aim to make the right conversation with the right people about the right topics.* That will mean a different target audience for each message or inquiry.

When laying out your strategic approach and securing funding, you will address the management team with a particular message packaged in a specific way. Deliver the high-level messages, never go into details. I know *my* eagerness to show my competence with the wrong level (too detailed or too high level) of information to the wrong crowd has many times backfired. All discussing technical details with senior management will accomplish is that it will take up the valuable time of executives and will always derail the conversation. The discussion may divert to areas you may not be fully prepared for at that time. Executives are smart people so they will often "know better" and will get bored quickly.

The last thing you want is leaving an otherwise good meeting feeling frustrated because you just spent fifteen minutes discussing what some technical parameters of a low priority platform are, and after you are sure you have done all the research and found the best solution, the VP tells you she knows a better way of solving that particular issue. Even if she is utterly wrong, that is a defeat on many levels. She will think you are incompetent, and you have successfully drawn her attention away from your past hour of productive discussion and some successful efforts you had presented. Don't do this to yourself. On the other hand, always have an elevator speech ready and know what you want to achieve when telling someone something.

Keep the technical details for the engineers, who on the other hand, will not be very receptive of some high-level strategy and scorecard design — they want you to tell them what parameters you want configured. Then they can tell you why that is not possible in their view, and you can begin the conversation to transform their *no* to a *how*.

Next to management and IT operations, another example of a security *market segment* is "all employees." It is the daily behavior of most of the end-users that will most effectively influence the security and control posture of the organization. So, in trying to instill "good behavior" across the organization, you will have to reach every employee, communicating different information, than you would, when addressing the CEO's concerns. So engaging the masses is also essential.

Marketing in the modern sense is whatever we do to find, or even create our market; learning about our current and potential customers, making enhancing their life our goal, defining why we do what we do and building our own brand. Your brand, or *why* you do what you do is what people relate to.[38]

Here is a lesson from the field of public relations and branding. Even though all three are the brands of the same company, "Lexus, Acura, and Infiniti are perceived as distinct brands, while the Diamante is perceived as Mitsubishi, likely due to the fact that they are sold in Mitsubishi dealerships. If something looks like a duck, walks like a duck, but is sold in a chicken-market, we call it a chicken."[39] That is an overly simplistic example and unrelated to information security. However, it is quite useful for us in recognizing a vital issue regarding the perception of security. Once a particular kind of perception of the IT or the security function has been established in your organization, as to its proficiency, efficiency, effectiveness, style, culture and added value, then it is essential to recognize it for what it is – good or bad. That is a challenge on its own, as turning a blind eye to a generally unfavorable picture is all too tempting. Even on a subconscious level, we tend to ignore any need for change, as even if the change would be favorable and beneficial to all parties, keeping the status quo is perceived to be less of a risk. The familiar ways of working and interaction — even if they are damaging over the long term — feel like home.

Once the true nature of our relationship with your clients (i.e., your broader organization, "the business") is revealed through your investigations, and it isn't the dynamic and open partnership you imagined, you must do something. Using methods well known to marketing and public relations, we must endeavor to turn our chicken into a duck, so that our organization's leaders would buy what we, as information security practitioners and leaders are looking to "sell" — and not something entirely different, or the opposite, or nothing at all.

Start with the Basics but don't Stop There

Security awareness, as it is done most of the time, is not capable of improving our human firewall anymore. We have reached the limits of the effectiveness of security awareness training from the last century. The one-way mass communication, to raise awareness of the importance and techniques of protecting information, is only capable of so much. Mainly as contents are often dull and not related to people's daily lives — either professional or private. Welcome to security engagement.

The level of effectiveness of securing the human element is directly proportional to the level of engagement we can achieve with our target audience, and there are several ways to improve that engagement.

Let's define three levels of engagement based on what Chinese philosopher Confucius said: "I hear I forget, I see I remember, I do I understand." The levels of engagement are thus: telling, showing, and involving. The first "passive" level is crafting an excellent basic end/user security policy and have people read it and sign it during on-boarding. Then have them listen to the same material in our presentations on awareness sessions in person or walk through it via e-learning. Better than nothing, a must-have basic, but far from being sufficient, of course, the main cornerstone of addressing risks related to people, is still a solid 'all-employee' security policy, frequently called an 'acceptable use and security policy,' AUP for short. In order to aid full understanding by an audience not primarily trained (or even particularly interested) in security, topics addressed in an AUP are best limited to those essential for all employees, with technical and procedural details left to be discussed in other documents intended for a smaller audience of those actually responsible for implementing security measures, such as IT or other supporting functions. As such, you better limit the length of the AUP to around ten pages, not more.

Spark interest

The second level, where we *show* what we mean, could be reached when we include elements of reality into our communication, using actual examples of what happened and, what can happen to our data and systems, and in turn, to our organization's services as well.

In daily practice, it is sometimes frustrating to realize that business or even IT expectations toward security many times do not readily exist as targets defined by our management. Issues are simply thrown over the fence for resolution. The first step is to realize how damaging that is to your effectiveness as a defender of the organization. Once you have recognized this, you can start working on the solution: creating the *real* expectation!

As the need for proper information security is not necessarily manifest in the minds of decision-makers, we have no choice but to see it as a product, or rather service, which requires a substantial marketing effort. That practically means that you need to find the place of information security within the life of your organization, and build up your internal brand. In building your brand, your goal should be to convey what you do and why that is important, ultimately make your internal customers want your service — protection. It is essential to recognize, though, that we build a brand through "PR" (public relations) methods, and maintain it through advertising, which directly drives sales. These two approaches combined is how we should approach the marketing of security as well.

In terms of information security though, that means that an ever so comprehensive security awareness training plan, or a well-constructed reporting system, just by themselves will not be very useful for winning over management and employees for the security cause. All practices detailed in different standards and methodologies for raising awareness are just advertising. They tell our audience about the security "product." Methods of good PR are significantly more subtle and usually focus on values and the why.

Keeping the personal "classroom" type of awareness training, for at least our key stakeholders, as opposed to just relying on the "magic" of e-learning tools — however fancy and comfortable they might be — is very much preferable. I am a great fan of automation, still. Here are some other examples of how we can make security a tangible experience with real-life examples for our audience.

The best approach to convey our message is to make it personal. Here are some questions to make things interesting — and interactive in a classroom awareness training setting:

- Have you heard of antivirus software (even though this term is becoming somewhat anachronistic when today we talk about endpoint protection)? People can be led to consider whether they have an endpoint protection software on their private computers? If so, why?

- Did you know that Social media services swallow, digest, analyze, and potentially sell all personal information you produce while using them? Not only what you type in, but everything you do, where you do it, even with whom. If something is free for you, then you are the product.

- Have you heard of celebrity data breaches? Photos and videos are made public without the consent and against the will of victims. The mobile device management solution the company installs on your device protects you as well!

- Have you ever lost your personal files due to hard disk failure? What was your "contingency plan"?

- And finally, a real eye-opener: Have you ever had your money stolen, via your weak password hacked on an e-commerce site, some purchases made in your name with saved payment card information that was not supposed to be kept there, then cancelled and refunded to the attacker's account so you can't access it anymore?40

Hackers are creative. Us, we are using gap assessments and frameworks to deliver dull lists of requirements and awareness training. I propose we don't just provide such basic content but aim to make users interested. Why not show how a hacker works? We can so easily explain the reasons behind our control measures, like more complex passwords or multi-factor authentication, when we relate them to the clever steps malicious attackers take to gain access to our systems and data — often through exploiting our human shortcomings. How a hacker works is potentially pretty exciting, and you can present it in a suspenseful way. Be unexpected, even foolish too! I have seen commercials talking about fruit juice made from "happy fruit." That makes no sense, people may laugh at the idea, but the goal of advertisements is for the ideas to stick in people's heads, nothing else.

Engage!

Phishing simulations, social engineering tests, or exercises of any kind such as enacting a crisis scenario like a widespread malware infection or DDoS attack, require more effort but are a great start in actually involving our audience, including decision-makers, and make them experience such an event, risk-free. The effects of a well-thought-out and coordinated simulation on the behavior of our users and management can be much more potent than just plain "telling."

We, as humans, are engaged and driven by good stories.[41] So, tell stories. In today's flood of Internet memes, we don't tell jokes anymore, which are the quintessential stories. Telling jokes share the same underlying principles as bestseller novels and great movies. It is worthwhile to study how some of the best-selling fiction novels are created and structured. Those methods applied to our communication can significantly improve our effectiveness as the vital ingredient we miss most of the time is making our audience interested and care in the first place.[42] Like I could tell the story of how my money was stolen through my weak password on an e-commerce site — one of the examples earlier (later refunded due to prudent payment processors). I wish I were better at storytelling. Don't you?

In larger organizations, HR departments usually have trained experts on how to communicate with the whole or a specific segment of your organization. They are trained in delivery, from crafting an influential newsletter, to organizing in-person events to facilitating more complex exercises. Why not have a chat with them and see how you can cooperate?

Keep at it

If you visited security conferences recently, I am sure you have seen guys on the stage, calling themselves "security evangelists." I must confess that sounded amusing to me at first. However, seeing the passion, these guys show when discussing different issues of our profession, made me think and ultimately change my attitude. What is different and exciting about this approach? Could this concept, borrowed from a religious context, help me, as a security manager to have more impact?

In brief, absolutely, if we figure out how and why evangelism is a thing today, in the form of technology evangelism and the like.

My conclusion is, that following the enthusiasm, and even borrowing some techniques of security evangelists, and evangelism in general, actually, will help us significantly improve our way of communications by integrating the following elements:

- Telling the "why" — the drivers behind your agenda — should come first
- Explaining the "what" — the story
- Bi-directional exchange — listen as much as, or more than you talk
- Constantly spreading the word — keeping at it, any time, all the time, anywhere and everywhere.

Evangelization does not mean just telling people to think or act a certain way. Of course, describing the "what" is essential. However, describing "why" is an even more critical part of the message! And even that is not good enough for us! Effective communication is always a two-way exchange among equally engaged parties, so our communication needs to involve active listening as well. It also needs to be constant to be effective. That may sound like something not even worth mentioning – and that is why it is so critical.

Keeping the flow of communication from and to the security team constant is one of the biggest challenges at organizations of all kinds and sizes. A smaller organization often lacks the organizational and technical facilities and rigor, to maintain a continuous security awareness program. On the other hand, the larger the organization, the more significant the challenge of coordinating and reaching each individual with our security-related messages. Why is that?

Keeping a continuous security awareness program alive is such a big challenge because the benefits of proper planning and execution, or the costs of neglecting this area are not directly and immediately apparent. No one will instantly share their password with everyone, abuse a corporate application, or steal data if they do not receive proper security education. On the contrary; the vast majority of our employee population will never breach security rules consciously with malicious intent. Frankly, those who do are not swayed by some speech. Managing the human risk of internal malicious employees is an area for another discussion. Our efforts in propagating good security behavior are most effective with "regular" users, who are benevolent, and would only be doing something wrong inadvertently, likely even without realizing it. Also, as the previously cited research shows, they are the overwhelming majority, so all this will be worth your while.

Our task to remind unwitting employees of the dos and don'ts regarding security is much like the job of an advertiser. Have you ever had the feeling that a particular television ad is "too much"? It was getting on your nerves, whenever you saw it, right? However, for sure it made you remember the product, or at least recall that you'd heard something about that thing — and likely, whether on a conscious or unconscious level, it had eventually influenced your decisions. Now, this kind of communication is annoying, but it works.

I have also seen end-users going crazy over a tablet computer offered as a prize to those who complete a particular survey from the security team. I firmly believe that gamified approaches and solutions will shape our future in terms of raising security awareness and employee engagement.

Imagine you are a singer or musician. If you don't have regular performances or release songs regularly, you will be forgotten. So, book gigs frequently!

So, now you know what the best time is to talk about security. It's all the time. Use every opportunity to talk about the subject. Or to ask about it. Should the answer to your question be 'No,' then learn not to ask closed questions, and more importantly, don't take no for an answer. Take no for a question!

NOTE TWELVE
on Persistence

"Taking no for a question"

SOMETIMES, DESPITE OUR BEST EFFORTS, we seem to go nowhere. That is normal, so to become genuinely unshakable in your approach, you must take no for a question.

When Your Best Isn't Enough

Some time ago, I attended a conference, where a very successful sports coach explained management practices around peak performing athletes. One of his comments stuck with me, which was that *adequately planned and executed work does not equal, much less guarantees, ultimate success*. That is a profound insight, especially for someone as nerdy as myself, expecting the deserved 'result' after completing a particular task following "the right methodology," each time in a predictable fashion. After all, predictability, or at least the illusion thereof, is what makes it possible to cope with everything life throws at us, right? So, when the result is not the expected one

– like successfully securing funding for a security initiative after compiling, tweaking, socializing and delivering a technically and financially sound business case – then that should be good enough reason to feel frustrated. However, that is precisely what this insight addresses; you may fail, even if you did everything 100% right – and this is not something to be frustrated about! The anecdote tells us that Thomas Edison tried and failed with more than a thousand ways to create a working lightbulb before he arrived at a working solution (note here I did not say 'the' working solution since there is not one single solution for any problem).

Why is this such a fundamental insight though? If you take not successfully funding a security project as a failure, then it is comforting to know that well, long-standing experience shows that failure may not be a result of *you* doing a bad job — failure may result from doing an outstanding job. You may say, *'What? There must be something wrong if the desired outcome was not achieved!'* The lesson may be different for everyone, and the sports analogy may not be fully compatible, but if you did your best — that's all that matters. The lesson is that there was likely a reason for not succeeding, and if found and addressed, there is a better chance of success. Now, what's next? Next is figuring out *why* things didn't go your way that time.

Opposers Turned to Fans

At one company, I inherited a project where we were in the design phase of introducing an integrated identity management system. One of the major roadblocks highlighted at the time by my predecessor was the HR department as they were reluctant to alter even the smallest part of their procedures, let alone start using yet another new IT system (our new identity management system) on a daily basis, so that our new system would have the information about onboarding of employees. They were resisting any change coming from outside of their own management circles, having zero apparent benefits, only additional work for them. The company was not a very large one, not large enough at least to have an integrated HR system, to which our IDM system could have been connected up to pull the new data automatically. So, the project effectively became stuck.

In my mind, there was no doubt that without the HR department's cooperation, one of the main input sources of the access provisioning process would suffer at the end, resulting in a broken solution.

Looking at the bigger picture, though, it turned out that the lack of a mature HR application and the daily struggles of the recruitment team would be a source of amazing synergies. After talking to the head of HR about the situation, and asking about their challenges, I found out that the actual employee onboarding procedure was still mostly a manual one, meaning sending emails, spreadsheets back and forth between departments, taking weeks for someone to actually "arrive" at the company.

As it happens, one of the fundamental functions of a proper IDM system is a workflow engine, which we were, of course, utilizing to cover access provisioning, revocation, approvals, and reviews procedures. After my chat with the right person, we realized that with a very much acceptable size addition to our scope, we would be able to include the HR department's onboarding process itself into our solution. Wow! After some management and project logistics, this was cleared, and we got the necessary approvals. What did that mean for us? We would not only obtain fundamental input into our new electronic processing system, but we would get it right at the source! What did that mean for the HR department? It was a transformation of a paper-based set of procedures into an electronic workflow — making their work way more efficient than before. I am happy to report that the implementation was a success.

So, what happened there? Basically, by looking at the organization as a whole, instead of just focusing on technology and *listening not just telling*, we turned a major conflict into a mutually beneficial endeavor, creating significant value for the company. After this deal, we'd transformed the HR department from a frustrated group of "external project stakeholders" to advocates of the whole project and the new system altogether.

For me, that experience was so valuable in so many aspects,

from value creation, service-based approach, selling and integrating security — but the main lesson in my mind is that a holistic and process-based approach yields a result where the whole can be more than the sum of its parts.

In my experience, the introduction efforts of any new solution, especially in the security area, focus solely on the technology aspect. The organization and processes surrounding the new tool are often not part of the project scope. That reduces, if not eliminates, any benefit gained from the latest technology — often the very reasons, the initiative may have been conceived in the first place.

The implementation of any technology will suffer in the absence of a parallel and tightly integrated effort to revise the ways the organization operates.

How to Take No for a Question

I believe that there are two ways of taking no for a question. First, you can keep working on the business case for your next security solution diving into details of the financial impact of costs and then realizing that you're stuck because you're unable to assign any positive cash flow to your solution. That is one of the inherent challenges with security solutions, and that's unlikely to change. You can use loss data from the past or rely on some fancy risk assessment to show the potentially avoided costs over the security breaches, but again that will not move the hearts and minds of management

Second, you can go back to the drawing board and learn even more about your organization, its priorities, and technical or procedural solutions that may be available to amend security measures, in other areas of business or supporting functions. Low level of interest from management may be rooted in a simple lack of understanding, lack of information, and the lack of context of your data. It's tough to come up with the top three priorities for security, especially if you are unaware of what the business priorities are. In practical terms, even the most basic security defense measures (baseline) must be built using strict prioritization based on risk assessment. To understand the organization and map its needs in terms of security, I find the SABSA business attributes quite useful. Instead of just three security "attributes," the CIA triad, there's a large number of "attributes." If you consider the line of business of your company, you will be able to narrow the list down to a top ten or top five list of security needs that will actually ring a bell with your management. Hint: that will need some structured discussions with them first. From there, proposing improvements to security measures is easy.

Childsplay

How long would you give an infant to learn how to walk? I guess you would not limit that time; children can take virtually any length of time to learn to walk, as their natural tendencies dictate. Not learning to walk is not an option (unless a prohibiting illness or other circumstance exists). Think about your goals in the same way. Is it an option, not to successfully close the IDM project, or successfully fund your program, or to be successful in adequately protecting your organization's information assets?

Now imagine you are playing a computer game (you may not be a gamer, still) and let's consider for a moment what games have to do with perseverance. Imagine a game that would end after your first failure to complete a mission, and you wouldn't be able to play anymore. That wouldn't work. The price of the game and your time would be wasted. Games have pioneered the concept of "extra lives." In a game, you would not give up until you complete your mission at hand. It does not matter if you fail three of thirty or a hundred times; you will likely carry on, and learn in the process, until you finally crack the challenge and succeed. And by cracking, I don't mean cheat codes.

Why would you have a different attitude in real life? Because of the risks involved, possibly. However, it's not like your life is at stake, more likely it's your ego. Maybe your job, but for that, you have to fail big time. So why not think of your job as a game? Your mission is to get into next year's financial plans with a new security solution. Or, your mission this month is to talk the IT operations manager into adding some steps to his process to cover a security risk. Who knows, you may discover some real-life cheat codes too.

Toddlers, when they fall trying to walk, always stand up again, and do not give up.

How many times do you usually try before you give up and either let it go or raise the issue with your boss (which never really helps anyway)? Why not solve it yourself? You will earn a lot of experience points on the way for sure, and find out that what you thought your best was, was in fact, just one step in your growth.

NOTE THIRTEEN
on Basics and History

"Use what you have to create an unshakable security program"

AS A SECURITY PRACTITIONER, it is quite easy to get overwhelmed by all the innovations, new attack techniques, and even the new directions your organization is taking. Security vendors, service providers and consultants are happy to push new and improved tools to cater to our (real or perceived) needs, to immediately address these new issues to give us some peace of mind until the next scare, in an endless hamster wheel of pain.[43] Before buying, though, (or getting frustrated by the lack of funding to buy) all the latest flashy tools, consider the following thoughts about what matters most.

Back to Basics

Like in life in general, getting the basics right, will go a very long way toward responding to any new threat or trend. The

Pareto principle says that 20 percent of what we do will eventually account for 80 percent of our results. A good fundamental set of measures will always make up the overwhelming majority of that 20 percent, whereas any new *distractions* offered by media, vendors or even your boss sometimes, will count relatively little and mostly fall in the other 80 percent.

Of course, this is a generalization. Being ignorant of current trends in terms of threats and defense, technology, and methodologies, in general, is not an option. That will slowly but surely put us on the bench in the security game. But, before that happens, we suffer several defeats as even though the 80/20 rule applies, we must still relate to the changing world around us. The key is finding the right balance between new and well-tried methods and distinguishing the hype from core issues and solutions.

The best way to deal with any new element in our threat landscape, architecture or defense is always going back to the drawing board and find where it fits our "security big picture"; i. e. our framework and architecture built based on for example the NIST CSF or ISO 27001. Never implement anything as a standalone solution, process, or technology, without creating links to the organization's and your current understanding of the world. If it does not fit in, it is either not relevant, or your security architecture needs a revision. Always make an effort to find out which one it is when encountering the security solution du jour. As a simple example, would you implement a web application firewall for a company that does not provide/use/host any Web based services? The question will never be so simple, and the answer will not be black and white. It is our job, though, to ask this kind of fundamental question: Is there a need and a fit for the new security widget out? Just consider: if you do not see how any security measure relates to your organization's goals and risk profile, who else will?

Let's take a practical scenario. Imagine that an organization falls victim of a denial-of-service attack. Hardly a far-fetched idea these days. As a result, they discover that their defenses in this area are not sufficient, so the security and IT team form a group and come up with an end-to-end "solution package," from preventive and detective technical measures to reactive and corrective procedural measures. In terms of "basics," two less than optimal things can happen. One situation, more directly illustrating our point here is that the organization does not have a formal incident management process. In this case, the new initiative (let's call it "DoS protection project") is required to design its own incident workflow.

Hopefully, this is never the case, though, unless it is a quite small organization. The other way you can make your life more complicated is simply not doing your homework and designing a full process around a single instance of one type of incident (i.e., the denial-of-service instance of the security type), and finding out only later that a robust incident management process already exists in your organization, and a few short discussions with the incident manager would have taken us almost to the finish line in terms of procedures by establishing just one sub-procedure of the overall incident management process, leaving us only having to be concerned about technical elements particular to DoS protection.

Again, it is unlikely – if not impossible – to find a larger IT organization without a defined and working incident management process, maturity aside. So, one can usually expect the basics to be there in some form. Also, that is another way to describe my point: you should always expect the existence and try to discover the relevant "good practice" framework elements already implemented in your IT or broader organization. If you look, you shall find. If not, then you have an actual case of your company not getting the basics right, which must be dealt with likely on a higher level of management. Either way, it is an essential trait of real security professionals to demand good basics from him- or herself, and the broader organization as well! That is a classic case of "think globally – act locally."

By the Book is for the Book?

Applying broader established frameworks to specific issues may seem bookish and artificial, even sound like consultant garbage. Reading article headlines such as "Mobile Device Management with COBIT" or "Cloud security with ISO27001" can evoke a doubtful reaction at first. After all, we do not manage mobile devices by waving our hardcopy ISO standard in the general direction of mobile users; we manage mobile devices with specific tools and solutions, right? Partially right. Any effective mobile security program will also include procedural elements.

What's more, technical solutions cannot be maintained, let alone sustained, without policies and procedures. One of the major hidden root causes behind the failure of technology implementations is ignoring the "soft" elements. To take it one step further, and bringing the idea full circle, I will say that in any particular situation, whipping policies and procedures into shape will get you very far toward your goal. In the absence of a new and significant threat, you may very well achieve your goals at any given moment, without actually purchasing new technology. Good basics in terms of how you operate will make all the difference in your effectiveness.

Applying good practice in a relevant and practical way to address weaknesses, ensures you have a solid foundation to tackle the constant stream of new threats. This way, you can do mobile device management with COBIT or cloud protection with ISO27001. From time to time, introducing new technologies is required for keeping our defense up-to-date, but often all you need to do is recognize that you walk the pretty much the same path (we might call it "implementation roadmap") each time some new threat or technology emerges. Only the scenery changes. So why not pave at least 80 percent of that path by relying on what you already have in place? Why would you reinvent the wheel, unless you have no other option?

Study History

Conscientiously discovering why particular things are done the way they are will yield valuable insight into how best to adopt your next solution in a specific organization, and how to identify and gain the support of key stakeholders. Become a student of company history, and world history in general, too. Not recognizing historical reasons, politics, results of organic changes and developments over time, will invariably result in resistance, resentment, and even sabotage to various levels. Introducing a new or changed procedure without respecting the context can cause the new process itself to perform under expectations, and likely even worse than the old one (or no procedure at all!), from the perspective of your stakeholders (i.e., the business and IT organizations). Also, keep what works, for even though the current satisfaction levels of the main stakeholders will likely not present a valid risk profile and capability levels in terms of security, but will, for sure, indicate major pain points, and, just as importantly, highlight what aspects of the security program *currently* satisfy your stakeholders. That may be the most valuable input to producing and executing a viable security strategy *for the future.*

On the other hand, to quote Machiavelli: *"There is no avoiding war; it can only be postponed to the advantage of others. [...] Severities should be dealt out all at once, so that their suddenness may give less offense; benefits ought to be handed out drop by drop, so that they may be relished the more."* That speaks to the contrary of the previous idea of treading cautiously but also contains valuable insight. Practice shows that even though management will not like too many changes unless there is a burning need or business opportunity, but will nevertheless appreciate the early warning, and a comprehensive picture which facilitates open discussion as well. Putting all "severities" in a package (or quarterly packages) requires that we do our homework and select the most impactful or beneficial security control improvements for the particular organization. Oh, and one package doesn't always literally mean a single big occasion.

Implementing another IDM solution at another company, I inherited the project about six months before completion. After two years of prior development, came the morning of go-live. The next day, the whole company's operation came to a halt due to the system's inability to handle the traffic and workflows going haywire, and I found myself explaining to the CEO. What happened? An IDM should not cause a complete meltdown of operations.

What happened was that this particular company relied heavily on people moving from one restricted area (and system) to another on a daily or weekly basis, often for substitution. That was modeled inside the IDM system and seemed to work just fine during testing. We did have some issues around the coding quality, but that, too, appeared to be fixed. So, in agreement with the CIO, we went live in a single step — and that was our fatal mistake. Replacing the old, rusty, but operational system with one big-bang rollout killed the whole operations for several weeks. Rolling back such a complex system takes several weeks, and until then, we were running on paper forms and emails. Half a year and some dollars later, we went for it again, this time with a phased approach, which worked. We still had some issues, but that is what phased rollouts are for — to allow us to correct our flaws as we go and not crash and burn while we do that.

Shaking Up but Remaining Unshaken

Finding the optimal level and pace of change is difficult, particularly when one finds him or herself in a new role. You need to hit a delicate balance between *disruption*[44] and maintaining the status quo. When initially encountering an organization, it is common to see a large number of practices, (procedures, methods, approaches) which appear to make no sense what so ever at first glance. The more experienced (and the more arrogant) the newcomer is, the more of what's happening appears nonsense. There is, after all, the right way, and the wrong way of doing things, right? Wrong. There is not a single good solution applicable to all circumstances. That is true for security as well, even if the frameworks, tools, and also the situation at our new organization appear to be identical to those we previously encountered. Experience is, of course, valuable, but it is quite rare to be able to apply precisely the same solutions as we did earlier, at a different company. The larger the organization, the more aspects will be hidden from the newcomer, at first, sometimes for several months up to a year. That is because of the annual planning cycle, for example. That one, you must go through at least once to get the hang of it at a given company! So, caution is advisable when — driven by the excitement of the new challenge — one decides on what and how to "fix" first.

Coming, Coming, Gone

Think of the cloud, DevOps, PCI-DSS, or the EU GDPR. These topics had been on the table for almost a decade, before quickly becoming top-of-mind problems due to a mandate or tipping point in market adoption. You listen to the same predictions on conferences for years and years, and then, when it happens, there you stand, scurrying for information. The contrary is also very true; if the time has not come, the idea will not catch on. The old wisdom holds that there is a time for everything. For sure, that doesn't mean that you will have time and opportunity to do everything you want. Instead, the message is that there is an *appropriate* time for everything. That implies that there are inappropriate times as well. To consider even further it is likely that there is a smaller number of good times and a larger number of bad times.

Choosing the appropriate time to do something may be the deciding factor for success. That means that even if all of the proper security measures are put forward for implementation, everyone may agree in principle but raise different concerns, some of which you may resolve by changing the timing. There are things for which the appropriate time is well known. These are things like when to submit annual budget plans (mostly in the late summer), when to respond to security inquiries from different stakeholders (ASAP of course…) or when to perform policy reviews (annually).

Determining the appropriate time to implement a particular security measure, however, can be more challenging. If we accept that security cannot work in isolation, that is. If we do, then we realize that it's wise to consult all stakeholders, especially sponsors. So even if the risk actually warrants a particular measure and it's also feasible, it is still very much worthwhile to find out whether the timing is appropriate for the organization. It is possible (though I don't recommend it) to come up with the security roadmap for the next couple of years on our own. Nevertheless, it's essential to gather feedback on the actual timing of each initiative.

They say silence is consent. When you walk through your roadmap with your supervisory or peer management team, and there's just silence, you may interpret that as consent, however, I caution against that. It may be a lack of interest. It's worthwhile to push for feedback. That is because you can only discover dependencies with other initiatives like business projects or internal process improvement plans in close collaboration with your management team.

Follow sound program management principles and map out the dependencies both inside and outside your security program. This discussion of timing is also useful to discover other priorities which may directly or indirectly influence the success of your initiatives. In other words, put yourself in their shoes. Possibly, accept limited scope — the limited scope is better than no scope at all. Then focus your efforts, like Lord Nelson.

PHASE FOUR

SUSTAIN

NOTE FOURTEEN
on Sourcing and Suppliers

"Caveat emptor!"

SO, WHAT IS REALLY GOING ON AT MY SUPPLIERS? That is a question you really should be asking a lot more! There is a tremendous push from business stakeholders to use cloud services instead of internally developed or even hosted applications. As protection activities are also becoming more and more dependent on tools and technology, the more push there is toward using external services to amend security measures. We are living in the age of everything-as-a-service, which drives not only the transformation of business strategies and processes but also the infrastructure they run on. And everything does include security services too.

Growing Dependency

An old argument in favor of outsourcing in general and cloud services, in particular, is that security is deeply embedded into cloud providers' core service, as a direct ingredient. As any failures and breaches in security directly influence their service, they do make security their top priority — as opposed to a "regular" company. Also, as that is simply all they are doing, they will be better at it than any organization focusing on their core services, which is rarely the business and IT infrastructure itself. Based on my experience with cloud-based providers, I find this argument quite valid, even though concerns about oversight and loss of direct control arise.

Also, security teams are not able to grow their size and experience that would be needed to oversee, let alone operate all the technology and digest all the intelligence and incoming information, so the security community is also moving toward managed and cloud-based services.

We are dependent on teams and technology outside our organization, and hence out of our direct influence. That is, in fact, a counter-argument against cloud services, but we cannot ignore the push for security to perform better and cover a growing amount of threats, which will only be possible by onboarding several external security services. You know, you are doing it.

That dependency is not to be taken lightly though. First, security vendors and service providers recognize our dependence and drive their own agenda. Any upcoming new threat means they can, and will, repackage their solution, whether it is a tool or consultation or a cloud-based service, and tell us how great that particular "old" solution is to handle the threat du jour. In 2018-19, the hype was about the EU GDPR. All providers of security services, consultancies, and others were jumping on the bandwagon, and have started telling us how their solution will make us compliant with the new EU regulation — from encrypted flash drives to database crawling tools to endpoint protection and next-generation firewalls, all across the spectrum. Each solution has its place in the security architecture for sure, but don't fall victim to those who promise all your problems will be solved if you adopt a particular point product or solution.

We will, of course, be adopting a number of security services as the anything-as-a-service economy further develops, some or most even based on or including cloud-based ones. So we better make sure we have done our part to ensure that our providers are in fact protecting our business the way we intend them.

With the broadening adoption of, and increasing dependency on external business and security services, the focus of security assurance must shift to include not only internal controls but also put greater emphasis on security measures at our service providers' and vendors' side and also on how we, as customers can gain assurance about the adequacy of those measures. That is true for external development engagements, but particularly important for cloud services due to ongoing dependency and some fallacies, such as the one that we can transfer accountability to service providers. We can't, really — in the end, we are accountable toward our customers.

You need to become a pro at defining and enforcing security requirements for suppliers. It's no coincidence that the 2013 version of the ISO 27001 standard and the NIST Cyber Security Framework both dedicate a whole chapter/category to security in the supply chain and supplier relations.

Let's look at the two main aspects of this issue: supporting business or IT in procurement processes and sourcing security solutions.

Supporting Business: Being strict but flexible at the same time

The first step in controlling the ever-greater exposure created by outsourcing and cloud solutions is to get a good understanding of your IT strategy in terms of cloud adoption, and external dependency in general. Often companies rely significantly on partners supporting particular systems and running the day-to-day operations of the IT infrastructure. Once we have a grasp of those exposures, we have a solid basis for regulating the control environment surrounding those. A good set of security policies and working arrangements with purchasing and IT organizations will enable security involvement, where it is needed to address risks early on. That is precisely the point where the security function can either be a roadblock, or a partner to find and flexibly address risks. Lots of options are usually available to solve a particular security challenge, and the best for all parties is when a real discussion and teamwork can yield practical but secure solutions. It is possible!

All too often, business solutions are put in place with minimal security oversight. Even though at a mature organization, the purchasing and development processes include security checks, still, as a consultant, I have often seen developments and system implementations where security functionality was reviewed only *after* they went live. That is better than nothing at all; still, there are ways to ensure we are there to raise the flag and at least have a transparent discussion on security issues early on.

Sourcing Security Solutions: The Proof of the Pudding is in the POC

While buying security services is essentially the same from a security point of view as buying business solutions, for security solutions, you are the buyer, so there are more options available to figure things out and select the best options. If you want to outsource or buy a service, you'd be better prepared to define it as explicitly and as unambiguously as possible, for the vendor.

Are you unsure of what kind of functionality and benefits you can obtain from a particular product or service? Ask for a proof of concept (POC) for free or a pilot, for a minimal investment, from the vendor. Usually, they are happy to do that as part of their sales process. These warm-up activities are beneficial not only for validating the product or service itself but just as importantly, the architectural and organizational fit as well. More often than not, vendors will use their "onboarding" procedure prepared for full-scale deployments, or part of it, for your POC or pilot. That is an excellent opportunity to learn. Such engagements are quite useful for vendors as well as they learn about your company and your industry, and frankly, sometimes about their own product as well. And who knows, in the end, all that may lead to the right solution. A word of caution though; these trial activities can burn substantial resources so be cautious about running such exercises for just any solution. Be selective about where you put your time and effort.

POC or Pilot?

What are a POC and pilot, and what is the difference? A POC is meant to figure out whether a particular solution will bring the envisioned benefits and align with your infrastructure and procedures. Usually, it is organized with development or test systems, and whatever is put in place for it, will be dismantled at the end. POCs are best done for solutions you have less information about, such as new kinds of products.

A pilot, however, should be planned so that anything created as part of it can stay in production after the activity, and be built upon going forward. That means for mature technologies and solutions, shoot for a pilot that can result in something lasting. A pilot is best considered to be the initial phase of a planned broader implementation.

A POC for an identity management solution may not yield additional knowledge beyond what you already know, so doing a pilot with one of your actual systems, where lessons learned, or even the infrastructure built can remain in place afterward, is potentially more beneficial.

Recognize and act on your organization's growing dependency on external suppliers, for core business and security services alike. Especially as cloud services are not just coming anymore, they are here, and they are here to stay, so you will be — if not already are — running on them for sure.

NOTE FIFTEEN
on Exceptions and Sustainability

"The time when everything works as you planned will never come!"

THE TIME WHEN EVERYTHING WORKS as planned — is the time you are out of a job. Basically. Preparing for, detecting and acting on unwanted events is at the core of good security, so I suggest you make peace with outlier events or exceptions, they are your friends. Your job isn't achieving zero irregularities; it's covering all bases and ensuring they are raised and addressed effectively — because they are there all the time.

Typically, at least a quarter of stuff does not go your way. Like 30% (or is it more like half...?) of servers cannot be patched in time according to policy. However, to recognize events and circumstances not supporting your goals, you need a defined baseline, embodied by sound policies.

Sustainability also means coming to terms with exceptions that remain after we eliminate wasteful (insecure) practices and introduced improved standards.

Create transparency

Publishing the security policies, starting projects, implementing processes will not solve every issue. There will always be exceptions, and that is normal. What you need is a way for managing outliers to your baseline requirements, which will be inevitably happening and will be happening about 30% of the cases. That means, for every rule, out of 100 instances, there will be about 30, which would go against your policy. That can be due to one reason or another, such as feasibility issues. Channeling all those exceptions into a sound *risk review and acceptance process* will create order in the chaos.

Management can transparently grant a shorter (few months) grace period or accept the risk for a more extended period, such as one year. That will enable everyone to focus on top risks. After that year has passed, for sure, the reasons that led to having to run the risk as it is will have to be reviewed again, and a new decision can be made, considering the current situation. Accepting an exposure in that way should always be preceded by looking for ways to mitigate it with compensating controls that may work around your challenges but reduce the risk somewhat.

If the number of exceptions to a particular security measure or policy is unexpectedly high, that may mean that a specific security measure is "too much" for your organization. That may very well indicate that you need to change your policy and improve the alignment of the levels of security to your businesses priorities and risk profile. That may mean compromise.

So it is critical to define your baseline requirements and then gradually discover exceptions. Taking a proactive approach, it is possible in three ways. Proactive means not waiting for and 'relying' on incidents or breaches occurring in our discovery. Let's review the three basic setups which are adopted in the majority of organizations.

Don't babysit every process

The first way to discover exceptions, which seems the most obvious but which is also the least efficient and mature is what I call 'babysitting every process.' That occurs on the 'first level' of control, which means having security representation in every relevant operational procedure, inside the process flow. That is like one of the guys in the following story.[45]

A small village had no water only when it was raining, so they hired two guys to bring clean water into the village. The first guy purchased two buckets and began hiking back and forth from the lake to the village several times a day bringing water. This process repeated itself every day with the guy making numerous trips from the village to the lake and back again.

The second person disappeared for several months and returned with a plan to build a pipeline from the lake to the village. They began to follow the steps outlined in their plan and built the pipeline for the next year. Once the pipeline was completed, the village had water 24 hours a day, seven days a week. Oddly enough, the second guy never hauled one bucket from the lake to the village.

Let's take the IT change management process as an example. Channeling every change, from minor to major, through a mandatory approval by competent security personnel is a very prudent solution. However, this approach has several weaknesses.

The first and most obvious one is that processing every change request indiscriminately will take up the valuable resources of the security department. We can then try to be more practical and mandate security review only for significant changes. That can work, but in that case, like when reviewing all changes, the security review will become a bottleneck. And that is the opposite of our intention. Besides, this way, we are sending the wrong message to the organization. *The message conveyed by the extra operational level check enforced by the security team, babysitting each change, every access request, may appear to be one of strict control, but instead, it is more about the inability to establish a proper governance structure.* This approach will also create a strong dependence on the side of the operations and other IT teams toward security checks.

After a while, the security check can become an excuse for delays and engineers will, instead of reading(!), understanding and applying security policies, turn to the security team to interpret every single detail of a systems architecture or solution, and make the go/no-go calls on a case by case basis.

For sure, if policies are not well written, are ambiguous or outdated, that may be the only way of keeping things under control. However, that leads to the fatal moment when the security manager lets go and forgoes all validation of what's happening; so it should be only temporary. All that goes against principles of good governance. Babysitting every process sounds too much like *hauling buckets* when you should be busy *building your pipeline*!

Audit solves all (not!)

The second and more appropriate way of discovering exceptions is through a regular audit process. Without going into details of that, it means that instead of reviewing every change "in line" as just described, we establish a formal schedule of reviews which will scrutinize one or more particular areas or processes, following audit methodologies. Simply checking and vetting each change based on evidence of operations, against an existing set of rules such as policies and procedures — after the fact, at the time of the audit. That may seem like losing control of the operational aspect, but it is actually the first "escape route" of over-burdened security teams to try and implement a kind of a balanced approach to oversight, where resources are lacking. That is how many of the internal "control organizations" operate in practice — using the work of others, as audit methodologies call it. In this case, though, it is the "others" — the security team in particular — are those, who use the work of the auditors to have more (or at least minimal) oversight of the actual state of the control measures.

Sustainable control

You probably know and apply PDCA. But do you really? The third approach embodies the cyclical approach to continuous improvement the best. It says that security validation of changes to the infrastructure and processes, (and all others throughout the organization) are best governed and regulated by security policies which are well written, well-known and practiced throughout the organization. Sounds like bullshit? Not if:

- your control requirements have straightforward evaluation criteria attached to them, and
- the first level of control (such as approvals and control activities like compliance checks) is consistently (and mercilessly) delegated to functional owners.

That way the dependency on you disappears and the security team can focus on what's called the second level of control; ensuring and validating that the control activities on the first level, embedded into procedures, is operating. Such an approach means a monthly, quarterly, semi-annual, or annual review plan to be formulated and executed by the security team. Coming full circle, findings from these checks would also end up in the risk management process, and be treated, or yes, may end up being accepted by management.

Sustainable services

I often see misconceptions about how advanced, or mature, security measures need to be. One of these misconceptions is that you must achieve the top capability or maturity level to be able to say you have proper security. However, that is not the case most of the time.

In my view, one of the main goals when implementing security measures and services is ensuring their sustainability. In other words, if we seek to introduce any kind of change, we also need to make sure it sticks with the organization. Very often, a particular security measure is implemented to fulfill a compliance requirement and viewed simply as a project. A project will end at one point and have a unique output, which is what we want. But as our goal is that whatever we put in place is not abandoned after the project, that unique output needs to include a set of processes or practices within the organization, that can be followed regularly by the designated owners going forward as part of their regular jobs. It's not an accident that all industry good practices and standards emphasize that we embed security measures into the business as usual activities. All the methodologies for security governance aim to build sustainable security measures. That is true even if they do it with different approaches, and the word sustainability itself does regrettably not appear in any of them, as such. At least you know now.

There is a good number of approaches to create the cultural basis needed for that to work, here is one as an example. Here is what the security or internal audit department can do. Introduce a regular check after audit findings presumably have been fixed to see whether or not the same control still exists after six months or a year. Initially, the results of these checks will be disastrous; about half of the controls implemented to address the audit findings will have been working for a couple of months or a few iterations, but then they will potentially disappear. After a few years of practicing such reviews and making the organization aware of the existence of those, results will start to improve. Implementing sustainable controls instead of just persuading auditors that everything is fine, becomes the default mindset across the organization — which is a great situation to be in!

Working to create sustainable solutions will be more difficult and time-consuming than just pushing things through once. You need to make broader arrangements with stakeholders and potentially make some deals for additional resources to delegate control activities to, outside the security department.

If you look at results over the long run, though, these efforts pay high dividends and also the discussions you have can become much more relevant to the business and have significantly more impact with decision-makers.

NOTE SIXTEEN
on Psychology and Motivation

"Human nature is behind it all"

WE ARE ALL HUMANS, from decision-makers in business and technology to end-users. That means that even though we may have a well-developed sense of business and financial priorities, or professional know-how, psychology always plays a role in every decision. So, what are some of the hidden elements of our psyche driving our behavior, often counteracting our protection efforts?

We Are Who We Are

Even though technology has been developing at a dizzying pace, particularly over the last century, basic human psychology and physiology have remained essentially unchanged over the last several thousand years.[46] There is a good reason for that; our genes carry our basic characteristics and abilities required for survival; patterns of behavior are defined mostly by our circumstances.

During the course of the last hundred years, we have just managed to integrate the fundamental achievements of the *industrial revolution* into our lives. Barely, I would say. In areas where we have seemingly succeeded, new problems emerged as the result of our adoption of a modern lifestyle. We are all painfully aware of all the kinds of physical and mental ailments caused by industrialized society, processed food, lack of physical movement, an overload of (irrelevant) information and other "conveniences" of modern life. After the industrial revolution, in the late 20th century, the *digital revolution* has begun.

As of 2019, this revolution is still mostly ongoing, having started only a few decades ago. Also, the pace of the change we experience is faster than any such change we have ever experienced, comparable to the speed of an explosion, especially compared to the much slower pace of change in the preceding millennia. Considering the rate of change, can we realistically expect the broader and broader masses of people using information and communication technology, to be already equipped to deal with the challenges of using it? That is impossible. There is a great multitude of technology-related, psychological, and other kinds of challenges to be overcome.

It is no coincidence then, that from malicious actors "Amateurs attack technology, experts attack people."[47] The phenomena and methods so well described by this statement are called social engineering. Social engineering sounds like a fancy "cyber-age" science. In fact, it is practically nothing but the exploitation of the weaknesses in our fundamental human nature, inherent trust (or gullibility?) and laziness to take advantage of us by using age-old techniques of manipulation and deception.

As the term "social engineering" appears so distant and esoteric to many people, this name does not convey the direct nature of the actual danger. Maybe if we use social engineering's other names; deception, scam, blackmail, fraud, hoax, con…?

Our sense of danger

Making matters fundamentally challenging is a subtle characteristic of human nature. There is a built-in level of risk we as individuals are used to accepting, and we, subconsciously, try to maintain that level of risk. That makes perfect sense when the level of risk increases, like when we drive an older car with used brakes and no airbag we will restrict ourself to a reasonable speed to keep our risk of injury at an acceptably low level. Well, most of the time, I guess. On the other hand, what happens when we get into a modern, well-maintained vehicle with airbags, anti-lock braking system, and a multitude of other safety features? Do we drive faster? Be honest. It is not to say everyone always speeds in a good car, but there is a definite tendency showing; according to research by Adam Shostack and Andrew Stewart, we do drive faster. To keep the level of risk, we are used to, the same over time, if, due to any reason that level of risk is reduced, that change induces a proportionate level of risk-seeking attitude. That is called seeking *risk homeostasis*. The same is true for information security. The more noticeable (and might I add: restrictive) the security measures, the more irresponsibly people will behave. Not because they are evil but because that is human nature.[48]

Consider any security solution, from a data leak prevention system to something as basic as a firewall. Properly implementing these solutions or procedures can lead to people becoming more careless in other related areas to "compensate" for the improvement in security. We do not want more protection than what we feel appropriate. The first challenge here is establishing the level of security our organization would optimally require. The second then, after having built a baseline of security measures is keeping what we have and not allowing good practices to erode over time. One requires clear communication with key stakeholders about security; the other requires a consistent control framework. Any security measure can have such an unwanted effect on us. In addition, if it is implemented improperly, the impact of the lack of expected protection is multiplied by the effects of our seeking risk homeostasis. Because of that, instead of strengthening our security posture, we may end up significantly weakening it.

From this, my conclusion is that good security is invisible. I encourage you to evaluate how visible, distracting, prohibiting your security measures are. As your goal I recommend aiming for the other extreme: Make security measures not hindering, but supporting, enabling operations — such as extending a workflow to cover a broader set of procedures inside an identity management system.

A Bird in the Hand

You might think that your management always makes purely rational decisions based on facts. Because of this, we go out of our ways to present risk in terms of tangible cost values which describe potential losses. The cost of security measures is supposed to be commensurate with that level of risk.[49] When we do this, the dynamics of convincing decision-makers is essentially the same as that of a discussion with an insurance salesman; we are advocating spending a smaller amount of money today, to avoid a more substantial expense (i.e., the cost of damage) later.

According to the utility theory of microeconomics, the consumer, (based on their preferences) will decide rationally when choosing the product better suited to their needs. In terms of security that would mean that virtually all proportionally sized (in terms of resources) security investments would get approved, as rational thought — and conventional wisdom — says: "a bird in the hand is better than two in the bush." That is, we'd rather spend a relatively small amount today than suffer a more significant damage tomorrow.

That is a fundamental element of conventional economic theory, and it supposes that whether it is a gain or a loss, our decision is always based on the level of utility. To illustrate the difference between the above common-sense expectations and reality, let's see the summary of an experiment, performed by psychologists Daniel Kahneman and Amos Tversky in the late 20th century. Take a roomful of people and divide them into two groups. Ask the first group to choose one of the following alternatives: they either *receive* an amount of 500 dollars with total certainty or 1000 dollars with just 50% probability. The other group is presented with the following options: *lose* 500 dollars with absolute certainty or 1000 dollars with 50% probability.

These two decisions are very similar. So according to conventional wisdom and micro-economy theories, both groups should reach very similar conclusions, regardless if it is profit or loss at stake -- there are simply those who gamble and those who don't. The actual experiment though showed a radically different outcome. When it was about profit, 85 percent of people chose the smaller but guaranteed gain (a bird in the hand). On the other hand, when talking about losses, 70 percent of people chose the uncertain but more significant loss.

The concept created by the above gentlemen based on the results of that experiment is called the *prospect theory*, and it recognizes that people relate differently to profit or loss. We have developed a dual heuristics in our thinking, which is fundamentally the following:

- First: a *sure gain is better* than an uncertain but higher gain. (a bird in the hand vs. two in the bush)

- Second: a *sure loss is worse* than an uncertain but greater loss. (live to fight another day)

These rules are dependent on circumstances; you would probably not accept ten dollars right now, instead of the possibility of winning one million with 50 percent chance later.

Nevertheless, everything else being equal, in case of a potential gain, we behave in a risk-averse manner, and in case of a possible loss, we are in risk-seeking mode.

How is prospect theory related to information security, and how does it explain the difficulties in "selling" security to our management?

It is the same thing; a choice, between a smaller, but certain loss (i.e., the cost of a security solution), and a more significant, but only "potential" loss (i.e., cost of a security breach). In case of information security solutions though, there is more to this decision; decision-makers need to be convinced of the potential benefits of our solutions, to start the conversation at all. Benefit or value, as such, as opposed to "simply" preventing losses is also a tricky concept, which we have discussed in the first part of this book.

Pain and Pleasure

All things considered, and all the risks presented, it is still more common in organizations to wait and see -- it's just human nature.

One approach would be to use fear. Fear (of pain) is an ancient instinct, much older than our capability for rational compromise. So if we vividly describe the implications of a security incident, should it occur, we have a much better chance to obtain funds for a security measure or solution that would prevent it or at least mitigate its effects to the organization.

That said, communication using fear tactics is not very ethical; in sales, it's actually illegal in most places. Also, most decision-makers expect more than a sales pitch based on FUD.[50] They deserve better, too!

Considering such psychological aspects is essential not only in terms of threats but also for successfully implementing our solutions. As behavior is also driven by experience, that is what we will look at next.

NOTE SEVENTEEN
on Ergonomics

"My security user experience... S.U.X."

HUMAN ERROR IS A TOP THREAT in the context of information/cybersecurity. About a quarter of discovered data breaches occur as a result of human error.[51] That means just direct result of human error. I wonder what portion of all breaches occur as an "indirect" result of human error – according to my experience, that percentage is much higher. Inside threats in general, including deliberate misuse and abuse, are of great concern as well.[52]

Security or functionality?

From our point of view, the ability to create value can be expressed in terms of usability, versatility, or rather the capability of security to support solutions and processes of other areas to be that way. The core question to address in this context is whether our security solutions support our organization's goals. It's a giant leap from being stuck in the constant animosity around "security versus functionality." Our users posting passwords on sticky notes under the keyboard because we enforce overly complex ones, is a typical example of common issues that scream for a better approach. It's up to you not to give up but rethink your strategy and find solutions which improve user experience to enhance the protection of your users' privacy, your organization's data, and operations. The answers you will come up with as the result of revisiting such long-standing unfortunate situations with ergonomics in mind will further *reduce risk while making life easier.* It will be no more security *or* functionality; it will be security *and* functionality at the same time! You can better protect business value by enhancing ergonomics.

Action and Reaction

People's experience largely influences their attitude and behavior toward any particular thing. It also impacts error rates. That is true for any interaction with humans involved. So, the most effective way to influence people's behavior towards something is to adjust their experience when they encounter that thing.

The basic principle of enhancing people's experience and the principle of *guiding instead of forcing* is best embodied by the discipline of ergonomics. Ergonomics has a key role in industrial and software design; user experience or UX design is a dynamically developing field. Helping and guiding people to do the right thing, as opposed to crude attempts at forcing compliance, greatly enhances effectiveness. Because what do we do? We provide "security awareness training" and publish guidelines on "acceptable use" and have people sign non-disclosure agreements — all in an attempt to educate, persuade or force(?) our colleagues to do the right thing (and refrain from doing anything wrong). These are all necessary steps for sure, but by themselves, they don't address the root causes.

As the nature of this encounter is such a critical element in determining behavior, you should do our best to make it a pleasant one. Otherwise, the effectiveness of your security measures and the realization of your security mission is in jeopardy.

An affair to remember

If there were just a single thing I could do to improve security, my choice would be the improvement of users' experience with security measures. Focusing on that alone will raise your effectiveness as a security officer, to a whole new level.

In our case, we are talking about our stakeholders' "Security Experience" (I like to abbreviate it as "S-EX" — much rather, than, say "S-UX," even though often the latter is more accurate...). Your stakeholders' experience is formed by the nature of their encounter with security, as a means to protect value.

What they face, however, is, more often a set of rules, procedures, a team of people, ways of operating, or a mindset in general.

Security and excellent user experience are considered to be
conflicting goals. That perception is not only wrong; it's harm-
ful. If security functions are not an integral part of a system,
organization, or process, you need to retrofit hardware, software, processes, or even whole organizations. So, users will
view all security measures as a hurdle and a distraction. On the
other hand, if something is ergonomic (i.e., designed for efficiency and comfort), it is also inherently more secure as a result, because humans are involved and with a well-designed
system, you can reduce their frustration, and error rate. So, if
usability is good for security, why is security bad for usability?
The answer is: security is bad for usability only if we ignore ergonomic considerations while implementing security. The approach to security, beneficial for all parties, is where these goals
are not in conflict. If we expect others to consider security during every phase of every lifecycle of everything, should we also
not consider other points of view in our approach to security -
such as ergonomics?

The Policy experience

Ease of use is a determining factor of successful adoption for
security mechanisms such as authentication but also policies.

If policies are easy to understand, there is substantially more chance of them being applied and followed. The briefer your policies are, the more effective they are.

Several times, I have had a fear of missing a particular thing in my "list of forbidden things" called the Information Security Policy. That fear of being unclear, or non-exhaustive, leads to our policies becoming long and hard to digest. Policies are often written as if they were spoken from a strict parent to a child. Restrictive, lecturing, and in the most terrible cases you can even sense the condescension of the author toward the "single-digit user." Similarly to a parent, security awareness efforts, coupled with policies, are more effective if their messages capture people on a deeper level, providing them meaningful reasons, easy-to-follow positive messages, and not merely prompting them to obey.

Policies and our security efforts, in general, should be aimed mainly at improving the behavior of our colleagues to make our everyday operations more secure. Now a very detailed policy may be convenient to make — it is, unfortunately, as compiling detailed rules is always easier than redacting the policy document to be comprehensible. Creating an effective security policy requires even more work, as we must distill the information to the level where it allows for audiences to relate to it, internalize the 'spirit' of the policy as well, and improve security themselves by changing their behavior willingly. Yes, there is an experience, which can hinder or support us, even with documents.

The world of UX design

The need to be secure does not necessarily have to interfere with usability. On the contrary, as some inspiring software examples show. Using ideas and methods behind ergonomics and UX design allows for much deeper integration of security into all kinds of entities from technologies to procedures, and consequently people's daily activities. That is precisely what we want to achieve, isn't it?

There are several UX topics[53] which, at first glance, have nothing to do with security architecture/management. However, they do, and your mission as a security practitioner (should you choose to accept it), is to figure out how. Some hints:

- Usability - make the life of your colleagues easier instead of harder, wherever security is involved. Protection is the end goal, but how we go about it, makes a huge difference!

- Information design and architecture - speak the language of your stakeholders, help them navigate the vast maze of information about security threats and defenses, so they can easily — and often willingly — adopt good practices. What you want to say is often not what you actually say and what your stakeholders understand may even be the opposite of your intended message.

- Branding and visual design - adopt a uniform look and

feel to your communications, even design a logo of your department; eventually, with the right approach, the security "brand" will be recognized, reminding people to be mindful of their actions, wherever they see it. Also, please, please, don't make your logo look like a police badge, padlock or shield! You can do better than that!

- Human-computer interaction (HCI) - last but not least, make use of good UX practices for security features in the area they were invented for: the design of the user interface and underlying security functions of business applications and security software alike.

Take action!

So, if after implementing all the technology and procedures you can afford, you feel there may be something more you can do to improve the security posture of your organization, go ahead and upgrade your colleagues S-EX. Focusing on ergonomics will vastly improve your effectiveness as a security officer -- yet this powerful idea is rarely found in information security standards!

So, get started:

- Establish your reasons for "ergonomizing." Don't accept all this at face value — as, without proper motivation, no endeavor will succeed. Evaluate security measures and solutions (or your whole program) as to their level of adoption and effectiveness. *If the level of adoption or effectiveness of a security measure is particularly low, it could be because of bad user experience.* Why not improve on that?

- Find some help. Any digitalization effort worth its salt will include the improvement of user experience as a fundamental component. Find the UX professionals on your digitalization team, if you have one, or software development team in general, and talk to them about your challenges in the effectiveness of security controls. Ask for their guidance on approaching the improvement of your "employee-facing" tools and processes you expect different teams to execute.

Evaluating and discussing your least effective measures that way will likely yield a list of improvement ideas you may never have thought of otherwise. Use that momentum to transform the image of your infosec function, and make your users have a great (and protected) S-EX — they may even want to learn more about it in the future!

NOTE EIGHTEEN
on Knowledge

"Plan-Do-Check-Forget"

TAKING OVER A NEW ROLE or starting a consulting engagement, I often wondered *why*[54] a particular team is doing things one particular way.

I have learned, that the real reasons for an organization, particularly an information security department to be at a given state at any given time, can not be recognized just looking at a point in time. Why things are the way they are can be realized only by investigating the plans and initial sets of actions of several, consecutive heads of security. The time of taking over the role, after all, is a time of putting a lot of effort in finding major issues, gaps and making comprehensive plans to "whip things into shape."

My experience as a security manager and consultant at different organizations shows that looking back over several years, the number of recurring security program elements is also remarkably high.

Plan-Do-Check-Forget

Some examples of these recurring elements, which are on the top of the list of every newly-appointed security officer:

- Performing (or at least chartering) a gap assessment against a major security standard, or the organization's security policies;
- Stabilizing/consolidating/reorganizing a few critical areas – usually in a "focused" (i.e., piecemeal, non-strategic) way;
- Formalizing/regulating information security processes;
- Addressing findings from internal or external audits;
- Being busy. That is not so much a conscious choice as a landmine you should avoid. It's always possible to focus if you try.

Those above are, of course, all quite valid considerations. The problem arises, though, when each new security leader approaches these challenges in entirely different ways. In a timeframe of six to ten years, an information security department may have as many as four different leaders. In unfortunate cases, key members of the security team may leave in rapid succession as well.

While these changes take place, something else noticeably happens. Noticeably, looking back after several years, that is! Freshly appointed security leaders, having very similar training and background, obviously identify very similar problems –

only, over and over again, every three years on average! The disturbing thing is that many times during these periods, efforts are *exclusively* focused on the major pain points — as isolated efforts, only treating the symptoms — and underlying causes of any sub-optimal operations or failures are left unaddressed. Likely, new solutions are implemented in many important areas. However, in the enthusiastic quest to improve the situation, the "old ways" of doing things are often almost completely discarded, and the real root causes of issues remain undiscovered.

Often then, with the eventual departure of the security leader, there is a very apparent decrease in the quality and performance of the security function. The practices built over a number of years while a particular direction was advocated and enforced, suddenly weaken. So instead of unbroken progress toward a more mature security organization, it is more like two-step-forward-one-step-back. Instead of learning, cultivating its knowledge and building on it – the security organization forgets!

Perpetual Amnesia

Unfortunately, such amnesia in the organization is not the exception, it is rather, very often, the rule; and that is the symptom of a pervasive problem. Security rules and procedures are not codified in sufficient detail and do not become part of the organization's everyday practices. Instead, a handful of key people are keeping things afloat, and if they leave the organization, the engine grinds to a halt due to lacking documentation and inadequate knowledge sharing and transfer. The result: the security team is forced to re-learn essentially the same concepts and methods over and over again in an endless cycle, every 2 to 4 years. So, the same ideas and initiatives, to *fix the basics* arise periodically – and then after some progress they are postponed or suspended due to different reasons from the security leader leaving to a new business/IT strategy overwriting previous priorities. A few practices may not become extinct altogether, but they suffer and deteriorate, due to the failure to maintain and embed them into practice in a relevant way originally.

A team is its own entity, separate from, but consisting of its members, so really safeguarding the knowledge and experience of the security team is quite impossible in an ad-hoc way. It requires the conscious use of knowledge management methods.

What do You Know?

The body of knowledge in a security team generally falls into two categories. One of these is the explicit professional knowledge, as codified in well-known industry standards, frameworks and the like -- even our policies. The main characteristic of such information is that it is structured and codified — ready to be consumed and applied. The other kind of knowledge is tacit in nature; this is the undocumented stuff; experience, background information, values, and in many cases, due to lack of formalization, even procedures, decisions, lessons learned of each colleague, our team, and other teams – these are what actually drive and guide daily work; "the way we do things around here". The problem with such tacit knowledge is that it can be applied in practice, only by the person who accumulated it, often unconsciously.

According to the well-known saying, knowledge is power. That encourages people to hoard knowledge, hold it back, keep their knowledge and experience for themselves, thinking that the information they withhold will make them irreplaceable. Unfortunately, the larger the organization, the more merit this point of view warrants in practice. In the *industrial age*, that is!

In earlier days, when information was not as readily available as it is today, the very existence of a particular set of skills or knowledge was often unknown and out of the reach of people starting out in a profession. That meant an additional layer of insulation for those hoarding their expertise as their less experienced colleagues couldn't even ask the right questions, so those "in the know" would appear untouchable. Not so much today. In the *information age*, anyone with a little bit of affinity can explore the basics of any topic. Recognizing the kinds and criticality of information, possibly withheld by others, is much more straightforward. That, in turn, diminishes the level of respect and protection the "hoarders" enjoy and leads to others becoming frustrated with them, instead of worshipping them. So purposely withholding knowledge backfires.

"Power comes not from knowledge kept, but from knowledge shared."[55]

A security professional learns, understands, and applies knowledge in particular phases over the course of his or her professional development. These phases go from knowledge to experience, and then, with more experience accumulating, generic, holistic understanding emerges, that makes the individual capable of making better decisions and act in new situations.

Learning *generic knowledge* is the goal of a student. To be effective in that, one first needs to *learn how to learn*. Until graduation, you study a lot of generalized things, which will allow you to function within an organization or team initially. Immediately after taking a job you will meet reality and start to accumulate *specific experience*. The more experience you gather, the deeper your understanding of the reasons why things work the way they do becomes. I call that *specific knowledge*, and *company-specific knowledge is among the most valuable assets of any team at any company!* To complete the journey, as you accumulate more specific knowledge, over time you will be able to predict better and better, how a particular situation would develop in the future, what outcomes you can expect. You are capable of that when your numerous different elements of specific knowledge merge and mature, over the years, into *generic experience.*

Ensuring Continuity

To build a stable security organization, acquiring, codifying, preserving, and sharing knowledge by integrating even basic knowledge management practices into your, your team's and team members' goals, is essential. Also, let's not forget proper compensation of key people.

Asking yourself the following questions can shed some light on how you are doing in this regard.

- Are there special, key persons in our team, keeping some systems or processes running? Are they key persons because their knowledge is specialized? Have they codified and shared it? If not, why not? Are they compensated sufficiently?
- Do we, or our colleagues, peers, senior management, and other stakeholders experience déja vu, when we propose something new? (They may not tell that to your face immediately, so just asking them can be quite revealing).
- Do we have a structured list/library of operating procedures? Is it maintained on an ongoing basis?
- Do we codify and share lessons learned?

- How fast can we bring people on board and align new-comers to our ways of operating? Is integrating new colleagues a new challenge each time or are there materials and defined steps for that (specific to the security team, of course)?

The generic and explicit knowledge found in the books is quite useless unless coupled with information about how a particular organization functions, and also why it functions that way. These two together are what you need to build a robust security team, the latter being the hardest to capture! However, that is what reinforces your team, and supports the members of your team to grow from entry-level analysts to senior specialists and from top specialists to mature generalists capable of functioning based on fundamental understanding — wisdom, on a team level!

ONE MORE THING . . .

If you found all this useful, please click the Like button!
Ahem, I mean… please do post a brief review on Amazon, to make finding this book easier for others!

Cheers,
Imre

ENDNOTES

[1] https://www.ted.com/talks/chimamanda_adichie_the_danger_of_a_single_story

[2] https://www.axelos.com/best-practice-solutions/itil

[3] https://www.iso.org/isoiec-27001-information-security.html

[4] http://www.isaca.org/cobit/pages/default.aspx

[5] In a 1950's speech former U.S. President Dwight D. Eisenhower quoted Dr J. Roscoe Miller, president of Northwestern University.

[6] Saul D. Alinsky: Rules for Radicals (Vintage, 1989)

[7] Single sign-on; a consolidated solution to identify and authenticate users across multiple computer systems,

[8] Quoting Harvey Specter form the TV show Suits, Season 2, Episode 8.

[9] Actually, centrally managed endpoint security solutions evolved from standalone antivirus products, which is a clever way to package additional security functionality. It started with the addition of host-based firewalls, file integrity solutions, data leak prevention and log collection and monitoring tools. The effect was that security and control software running in separate threads on clients and servers began taking up a noticeable amount of CPU power and memory, impacting host performance. Then security vendors began packaging all that additional functionality into single agents, somewhat alleviating this issue, but also, just as importantly, providing more comprehensive protection. In this case, additional business cases were not needed, we were able to focus on technology implementation and organizational adoption.

[10] https://cmmiinstitute.com

[11] https://sabsa.org

[12] Luftman, Jerry: Assessing Business-IT Alignment Maturity, Communications of AIS, Volume 4, Article 14, December 2000

[13] In his 1989 book, "The 7 Habits of Highly Effective People", Stephen Covey describes the "maturity levels" of humans as "dependent, independent and interdependent — the latter being the most advanced, as at that level of development you are able to listen first, think in terms of win-win, and find synergies with your partners. The concept applies to organizations as well, in particular for our purposes, the security department.

[14] A great example is a bank educating all their customers (via a newsletter, for instance, or on their website) about the risks of phishing attacks and how to defend against them.

[15] Andrew Jaquith: Security Metrics: Replacing Fear, Uncertainty, and Doubt (Addison-Wesley Professional, 2007)

[16] *"All animals are equal, but some animals are more equal than others." — George Orwell: Animal Farm*

[17] Lenny Zeltser, 2009

[18] The AIDA model has been elaborated by a number of marketing minds, but the first actual mention, with the specific steps in this order appeared in an article by C.P. Russell, "How to Write a Sales-Making Letter," Printers' Ink, June 2, 1921

[19] APTs are a stealthy type of cyberattack, which may be undetected and occur during an extended timeframe.

[20] https://corporatefinanceinstitute.com/resources/knowledge/other/aida-model-marketing/

[21] https://www.emvco.com/emv-technologies/contact/

[22] Eva Keszy-Harmath, 2009

[23] Banning a new technology or solution perceived to be useful by the business decision makers or the user population never works in practice. There will always be exceptions.

[24] Fundamental investors look at the basic vision of a company, along with key financial information, operational data, market position, etc. - taking a long term perspective, as opposed to investors relying

on mathematical/ technical analysis of stock price charts.

[25] Shark Tank is a US TV show where investors grill candidates, who are pitching to them, aiming to receive investment in their businesses. Watching it is thoroughly recommended.

[26] CAPEX vs OPEX preference, internal FTE or contractor preference, etc...

[27] https://www2.deloitte.com/content/dam/Deloitte/us/Documents/risk/us-risk-black-market-ecosystem.pdf

[28] 2018 Cost of a Data Breach Study by Ponemon - https://www.ibm.com/security/data-breach?

[29] A saying attributed to Mark Twain

[30] The ITIL V3 Service Strategy book offers the following definition of a process, which I consider to be accurate, even if incomplete. It says: "Processes define actions, dependencies and sequence". (ITIL actually offers a number of definitions, but this one appears to be the most practical.)

[31] Processes defined "from start to finish" covering the entire lifecycle of an end product or result, across departments and organizations, internal or external.

[32] Being "pwned" was derived from "owned" means being utterly defeated, or in terms of security, being compromised or controlled by an attacker.

[33] The structured allocation of roles in terms of who is Responsible, Accountable, Consulted or Informed. This approach has many flavours and is worthwhile to research due to its effectiveness and practical usability.

[34] Auditablity is basically the ablity to create records for traceability. Logging when someone clicks an approval button is such a function.

[35] https://iapp.org/news/a/data-indicates-human-error-prevailing-cause-of-breaches-incidents/

[36] Phishing is an e-mail-based attack technique attempting to obtain sensitive information from the user directly by disguising the attack as a legitimate message.

[37] The success rate of phishing attack is the rate people respond to it in some way, opening attachments, clicking on links, even entering authentication or other sensitive information at request.

[38] Simon Sinek: Start With Why (Portfolio; Reprint edition, 2011)

[39] Al Ries and Laura Ries: The Origin of brands (Harpers, 2005)

[40] Too specific? Yes, that's a personal experience that taught me a few lessons.

[41] Check out Andrew Stanton's TED talk called: The clues to a great story

[42] https://www.well-storied.com/blog/3-awesome-plot-structures-for-building-bestsellers

[43] Andrew Jaquith: Security Metrics: Replacing Fear, Uncertainty, and Doubt (Addison-Wesley Professional, 2007)

[44] rapid and unexpected change

[45] Adapted from: Robert Kiyosaki: Rich Dad's CASHFLOW Quadrant: Rich Dad's Guide to Financial Freedom

[46] http://human.projects.anth.ucsb.edu/epfaq/holocene.html

[47] Bruce Schneier: Secrets & Lies - Digital Security in a Networked World (Wiley, 2000)

[48] Adam Shostack and Andrew Stewart: The New School of Information Security (2008, Addison-Wesley)

[49] My personal opinion is that you should spend no more than 30% of what you perceive as value at risk at any time. Defining the level of risk in quantitative terms is quite difficult too, and impractical in my view. In particular, establishing "probability" or "frequency" is next to impossible because whatever happened in the past may not happen in the future.

[50] fear, uncertainty and doubt

[51] https://securityintelligence.com/ponemon-cost-of-a-data-breach-2018/

[52] http://info.kroll.com/e/37972/n-us-fraud-report-confirmation/58dck8/550392685

[53] http://deviseconsulting.com/defining-ux/

[54] This is a different "why" than previously discussed, we are not looking for the ultimate goal and the reason for existence, but the circumstances that lead to things being the way they are today.

[55] Bill Gates: Business @ the Speed of Thought: Succeeding in the Digital Economy (Grand Central Publishing, 1999)